LET GO, LET GOD

John E. Keller

AUGSBURG Publishing House • Minneapolis

LET GO, LET GOD

Scripture quotations unless otherwise noted are from the Holy Bible: New International Version. Copyright 1978 by the New York International Bible Society. Used by permission of Zondervan Bible Publishers.

The Twelve Steps of Alcoholics Anonymous on pp. 74-75 are reprinted with permission of Alcoholics Anonymous Services, Inc., copyrighted 1939, 1955, 1976.

The quotations from *The Spirit of Cardinal Bernardin* on pp. 104-107, © A.E.P. Wall, are reprinted with permission of The Thomas More Press, Chicago IL 60610.

Library of Congress Cataloging in Publication Data

Keller, John E., 1924-
  Let Go, Let God.

  1. Christian life—Lutheran authors.   2. Alcoholics.
3. Alcoholics Anonymous.   I. Title.
BV4501.2.K423   1985   248.4'84131   85-11048
ISBN 0-8066-2162-1

Manufactured in the U.S.A.   APH 10-3815

                    0   1   2   3   4   5   6   7   8   9

To my father, Pastor W. W. A. Keller, who provided the early personal relationship and the teaching and preaching of grace and trust within the Christian message that make up the roadbed of this journey.

To my wife, Doris, who more than anyone else provided the relationship essential for ongoing personal integration, change, and growth related to the material in this book, and gave of herself in many ways, including the willingness to make the various geographical moves that were a part of this ministry.

Contents

Acknowledgments

Within this book is a debt of gratitude to the American Lutheran Church for calling me to specialized ministry in alcoholism and to Alcoholics Anonymous, which not only was the primary source of learning about alcoholism but became the paradigm on my journey of integrating religious beliefs and clinical understandings outside of as well as within the Christian message.

A special word of acknowledgment for my deceased friend and colleague, Dr. Nelson J. Bradley. If it were not for his awareness, acceptance, and integration of the spiritual reality as found in Alcoholics Anonymous into the understanding and treatment of alcoholism, there would never have been this specialized ministry, which began with training under his leadership at Willmar State Hospital, Willmar, Minnesota, in 1955.

Two pastors, Luthard Gjerde, D.D., and Fredric Norstad, D.D., were the persons through whom this ministry was initiated within the church through Lutheran Social Services of Minnesota.

I also want to express great appreciation to Geri Jonas for her willing spirit and amazing patience in typing numerous drafts and corrections of this manuscript, to Grace Valenziano for typing final revisions, and to Nancy Scovill, who, in typing a series of meditations on grace and human limitation, said that someday I needed to include their content in a larger manuscript. That happened in this book.

Preface

When I accepted the call to specialized ministry in alcoholism in 1955, it was not only the beginning of a journey in seeking to understand alcoholism for the church, but the beginning of a journey into a much broader realm. It brought me into an environment in which spiritual reality was integrated into the professional treatment of people with alcoholism. It brought me into an environment in which psychiatrists, physicians, psychologists, and other clinicians understood and accepted the spiritual dimension of human existence.

It has been a 30-year journey in seeking to understand the nature of the spiritual in the human condition and in human relationships, to integrate religious beliefs and clinical understandings outside of as well as within the Christian message, and to integrate the spiritual in the care and healing of people. You are invited to share in the journey.

There is no life without pain, brokenness, and limitation. This is our common human dilemma. This book requires that you face the reality of physical, emotional, and spiritual pain. It requires that you face the reality of your own brokenness, the brokenness of others, the lack of wholeness in human existence. It requires that you face what Ernest Kurtz calls "essential human limitation." This book does not require that you face it grimly, but it does require that you face it realistically.

This book also requires that you face the reality of faith, perhaps your own personal faith. Just as there is no life without pain, brokenness, and limitation, so there is no life without faith. Atheism is a faith; agnosticism is a faith; every religion is a faith. This book addresses our common human dilemma and the relationship of faith to these aspects of the human condition. How do you live with the pain, brokenness, and limitation in your life, in the lives of others, and in your life together with others? What does your faith have to say to these realities?

This book is not idealistic regarding human potential. It is not another book on self-improvement and self-success couched in the language of religion or psychology. Nor is this a book of moralistic answers. Rather this is a book that invites you to share in the journey of one person, together with others, a journey in which I have come to an abiding faith that meaning, hope, and fulfillment can be found only within and through the pain, brokenness, and limitations of life

To come along on this journey you do not need to be involved in any religious faith. Atheists and agnostics have been fellow travelers and friends along the way. At no time will you be preached at or moralized with. Your personhood and personal integrity will not be tampered with or violated. If your journey makes it impossible for you to identify with my journey, neither of us will be diminished, but I hope that in sharing the journey we will meet each other in our common humanity, if not in our faith.

On this journey I have learned that religious terminology, particularly Christian terminology, can trigger a variety of negative perceptions, feelings, and reactions, even among people raised in the church. Some of that is related to distorted perceptions learned in religious education. Some of it is related to having been unheard, misunderstood, and moralized with and rejected by religious teachers— parents, pastors, or members of religious communities. Some of it is related to painful, tragic, unreasonable loss in life for which no healing was experienced. And some of it seems unfathomable.

If you tend to react negatively to religious language, you are encouraged to continue on the journey, to keep reading at least for a while. I hope that you will sense in this book our common ground in the human experience, for in so much of the journey in life we are together, whether we are aware of it or not.

There will be the language of the Christian religion in this book. Some may find that their understanding of its meaning will be changed. Indeed, that is one of my hopes.

In this journey the spiritual dimension of human existence is accepted as a given and is positively affirmed. This book is concerned with spirituality in life both outside of and within religion. In seeking to understand and communicate spirituality the non-religious paradigm of A.A. is used; it then serves as a lead into the meaning of the Christian message in relationship to our common human dilemma.

In one way my journey is different from the journey of many others. I have experienced very little physical pain, but I have spent considerable time with people in severe physical pain and with some over long periods of time. I recall some who despaired and others who endured such pain without any meaning. I also recall a man who symbolizes many others on the journey. He was in his late 50s, dying a slow death with terrible pain from cancer. Each time I left his hospital room, I was aware of having received more from him than I had been able to give, of being astounded by his gratitude, his enduring patience in suffering, and his abiding faith in Christ.

Most of the personal pain, brokenness, and limitation in my journey has been emotional and spiritual. And much of the content of this book comes from the past 30 years of the journey, beginning with the acceptance of the call to full-time specialized ministry to alcoholics. Alcoholism brings with it some of the severest experiences of pain, brokenness, and limitation both for the alcoholic and the family. It is their experiences that serve as the paradigm for spirituality in this book, particularly as it is expressed in the nonreligious fellowship of Alcoholics Anonymous.

CHAPTER ONE

Pain, Brokenness, and Human Limitation

All of us experience pain—physical, emotional, and spiritual. Looking at, reflecting on, and experiencing such pain is not enjoyable. Nevertheless, pain is a reality for all of us, alone and together. Therefore, it is not only important, but essential, that we look at and reflect on the pain we experience.

The Search for Meaning

There is no completely satisfying answer to the reality of pain, especially the *why* of pain. If you don't believe in God, pain is a harsh inevitable reality of life with no meaning. If you do believe in God, inside or outside institutionalized religion, your faith only raises more questions about the pain reality. You may believe in a God who deliberately chooses to punish because we are sinful people, but then why is God like that, and why do you want to believe in such a God? You may believe in God, as revealed in

Christ, as a loving God, but then why did such a God create a world and people in which he knew there would come pain? Doesn't that ultimately make God responsible for our pain? Or does it? If it doesn't, then why did God create us in such a way that we could bring pain into life? And certainly we can't be responsible for earthquakes, tornadoes, drought, floods from heavy snow melting or downpours of rain, or destruction caused by other forces of nature? There are accidents for which no one seems to be responsible. A person has a heart attack while driving, and people are killed or permanently disabled. An unidentified genetic factor results in a child being born with a physical handicap. Whose responsibility is that? And if a loving God created us and allowed for imperfection to become a reality, there will always be accidents and pain of various kinds because of human imperfection. For the believer or nonbeliever, the believer in a punishing God or a loving God, the questions go on and on.

With all the questions, pain remains both a reality and mystery on our journey through life. Somewhere deep inside us we need the hope that, given the reality and mystery of pain, there can be meaning and hope for us, both alone and together.

Our Common Human Dilemma

Now take a deep breath as we have our first look at human pain, brokenness and limitations in brief descriptive form. It is obvious that many people experience a lot of fun, enjoyment and satisfaction in their lives together with others in the family, in friendships, in work, in service to others, in recreation, in entertainment, in vacations and in celebrations. But many in the world don't. It is obvious that many experience the goodness of others, the goodness of honest, open, warm, emotional relationships, the goodness of the earth, the beauty of nature, and the wonders of the universe. But many don't.

All people in the world experience pain, brokenness, and human limitation—both alone and together. With birth comes aging, separation, and dying, with many dying prematurely. Accidents, some avoidable and some unavoidable, hurt, maim, and kill. There are incurable diseases and medical conditions, mental and physical disabilities, hunger and hopelessness, and human and material destruction by uncontrollable forces of nature, carelessness, and defective mechanisms.

People feel misunderstood, inadequate and inferior, invulnerable and superior, alone, guilty, and rejected. People practice dishonesty with self and others. They experience conflict in marriage, in family, and in friendship, conflict at work, in society, and among nations. There is desire for power and domination of others by overt or subtle actions. All these realities—personal, societal, and global—cause us pain over which we have no control but want control. We desire to control the attitudes, feelings, and behaviors of others that cause us pain—but we cannot. We desire to control all the realities within the self that cause us pain—but we cannot.

Many experience the pain of racism and bigotry. Some positive changes have taken place in our society for blacks because courageous individuals like

Martin Luther King Jr. and Rosa Parks spoke out. Their actions resulted in organized social responses that produced change. But we still have a long way to go in providing blacks and other minorities with educational and vocational opportunities, greater inclusion in the political process, and adequate nutrition, health care, and housing. We can feel grateful for the change that has taken place, but many still live with the pain of racism and discrimination.

We all face the pain of large-scale violence. Along with the benefits of our ever-expanding knowledge and scientific capability comes the potential for greater evil and destruction. With increasing potential for saving, enhancing, and prolonging life, we have also the unbelievable, unimaginable capability of destroying human life and all forms of life through nuclear power, pollution, and by just general poor stewardship of the earth's resources. And for us all there is the terrible threat of nuclear war.

Although we have greater understanding of the essentials for healthy, meaningful relationships, one out of two marriages in the United States ends in divorce. Many other marriages will not end in divorce, but lack a meaningful, satisfying, fulfilling relationship. Serious effort is required if a marriage is to be increasingly satisfying, with ongoing individual and mutual growth. It doesn't come naturally or easy; it comes with pain. Serious problems in the relationships between parents and children are forever in the news. And we demonstrate no significant progress in learning how to live together within a nation or as nations in a meaningful, harmonious manner for the good of all.

At the beginning of the 20th century many were optimistic, believing that democracy would be the hope of the nations and that nations would learn how to live together in trust for their mutual good. Then to our dismay, a war had to be fought to safeguard democracy—then another more global war. Then there was the Iron Curtain and Vietnam, the Middle East and Central America. The human capability for evil and pain proved astounding and irremovable, yet today we attempt to keep it in check by nuclear threat.

Pain, brokenness, and human limitation are our common human dilemma. No one escapes—neither individuals, societies, nor nations. No one is invulnerable. In the midst of these realities individuals, societies, and nations are born and live. We all are confronted with fundamental human questions: What do you do with the pain, brokenness, and limitation in your own life, in the lives of others, and in your life together with others? What does your faith have to say to these realities?

CHAPTER TWO

The Paradox of Denial, Escape, and Attempts to Heal

Life has many paradoxes. A paradox is two statements or behaviors that seem completely contradictory yet together are true. One paradox that is present in every human journey is the effort to try to heal while at the same time denying and trying to escape from the pain, brokenness, and limitation in our lives. Often this is done at the unconscious or subconscious level and involves considerable self-deception. On my journey I came to see alcoholism as a paradigm of this behavior, demonstrating that we can neither *escape from* or by ourselves *heal* our own pain, brokenness, and limitation.

Because of the pain, brokenness, and limitation in life all of us experience varying degrees of anxiety or *dis*-ease in our relationship with self, others, and with God (or the absence of God). For some people, for reasons not yet understood, alcohol intake has a magical, almost instantaneous effect on those feel ings. Those distressful feelings are not only gone but are replaced by extremely good feelings.

A man who thinks he has three feet, can't dance, and no woman would want to dance with him, has a few drinks. All of a sudden he is the best dancer around, and all the women would want to dance with him. He is on top of *his* world, but more than that, he is on top of *the* world. A woman feels inadequate and unfulfilled as a person, wife, and mother. She also experiences discomfort in social situations. Then she discovers that alcohol removes all that pain. It's like magic for her. Her perception of herself as a person, wife, and mother becomes positive. She feels confident and comfortable in social situations.

These two people have experienced temporary escape from and healing for the feelings that spring from their pain, brokenness, and limitation. They feel they have found life, wholeness, and fulfillment through the anesthetic effect of alcohol. They may not think about it in that way, but they feel and experience it.

A young person is socially uncomfortable, has low self-esteem, and doesn't feel he belongs. By getting involved with drinking and drugs he not only begins to feel a sense of belonging, but his feelings about himself and others are dramatically changed. He thinks everyone has the same kind of transforming experience. Because of this experienced effect of alcohol and other drugs, he thinks this is "life" for him.

Alcohol works for some people, why we still don't know. But it appears that a rather small percentage of those who drink get such a special effect. For them it works so well that even the skid row alcoholic can remember how wonderful it felt, even though he hasn't been able to get that effect for many years. It works so well that the pain in alcoholism can be so easily forgotten and the wonderful effect from alcohol so readily remembered. Nothing and no one has ever provided anything to compare with that transformation, that new perception of self and life, that comfort with others, that feeling of being acceptable and accepted, that absence of pain and anxiety, that healing, that finding of life—even though it is temporary.

Whenever the alcoholic takes that first drink again, the desire and intent is to get and keep that effect—to escape, and yet experience healing, wholeness, and fulfillment. In this sense alcoholism is a spiritual quest. But because alcoholism is a permanent and progressive loss of control over the drinking—a primary reason for alcoholism being classified as a disease or illness—there comes the increasing inability to gain or maintain that effect, and the drinking enlarges and intensifies personal, marital, family, social, spiritual, vocational, and health problems. More and more of life is literally lost. Pain, brokenness, and human limitation are increased. Alcoholism provides a dramatic portrayal of seeking to save your life from the pain, brokenness, and limitation—and in the process losing it.

Denial, Rationalization, and Blame

To have this paradigm be of value for us who are not alcoholic, we need to identify and accept the ways in which our common human pain and dilemma find expression in our lives. We can begin by looking at the behavior that is frequently identified as "alcoholic behavior"—the denial, the rationalizing of the drinking, and the blaming of it all on someone or something else. That, of course, is not only alcoholic behavior; that is our common human behavior. That is the natural human reaction to pain, brokenness, and limitation. It is as old as Adam and Eve. Whether you believe that story literally or as a myth or not at all, it profoundly describes our behavior: "It wasn't me; it was the woman you gave me." "It wasn't me; it was the serpent."

How natural and easy to *deny* negative realities about ourselves, to *rationalize* unhealthy attitudes, feelings, and behaviors to ourselves and others, or to *blame* them on someone or something else. These are natural behaviors when someone hurts us or we hurt someone else, when our imperfection and limitation are evident. We seek our way out from the reality and pain of it all.

An element in this behavior is different for alcoholics than for many nonalcoholics. In alcoholism these reactions become a system of behavior that controls and dominates the person. They become *the lifestyle* rather than just a part of life. Alcoholics become so locked in with these kinds of behaviors that they literally can't see their alcoholism. This same thing happens in certain psychiatric conditions. People become so dominated by denial, rationalization, and blaming that they are not able to see the reality of their condition. That's another reason why alcoholism is called an illness or disease. Alcoholics become unable to behave any other way in regard to the alcoholism until they receive outside help.

But all of us exhibit these behaviors as reactions to our common human condition. We deny, rationalize, and blame. These behaviors are helpful for enabling us to see that in simple, common, automatic ways we all try to escape from and at the same time gain some sense of healing for the pain of our brokenness and limitation.

In addition to looking at these human behaviors which are common to us all, we also need to become aware that in all of our lives there is a tendency toward other *nonchemical* addictions. We need to look at other manifestations of addiction so that those of us who are not alcoholics can say, "That's me."

In the early 1950s, Dr. Nelson J. Bradley, a psychiatrist and pioneer in alcoholism treatment, began lecturing about other human conditions and behaviors that in many aspects were similar to alcoholism. If you can't identify with alcoholism, see if you can identify with any of the following. You may not be involved in any of these other addictions, but try to focus on the behavior, on the human striving for both escape and healing, and how it may be expressed in your life.

Addiction to Success

People can be successful but not be success addicts. However, success addiction is extremely common, and unlike alcoholism, it is, unfortunately, highly rewarded. Quite often with success addiction there is power addiction and almost always work addiction. Some people get a high from success like the effect others get from alcohol. You hear it when you listen to them. You are struck by their seemingly endless store of energy. Success works wonderfully well for some. They experience an escape from and a perceived healing of the pain, brokenness, and limitation of life, without being aware of what they are experiencing. Just as with alcohol, why success works so amazingly well for some people in relationship to the human dilemma, no one knows.

Success is even a more deceptive god than alcohol, because the results and rewards within vocation and society give clear messages that success is the healing of pain, brokenness, and human limitation, that success is life itself. But the person addicted to success finds that he or she can never be successful enough. With every success the success-addicted person is left with the same unresolved internal realities as the alcoholic. As with alcoholism the behavior of the success addict becomes predictable, stereotyped, and repetitive. The person is locked in and dominated by success. Like alcohol, success can't heal or give meaning to the human dilemma. The desired applause and reward can never be sufficient and can never be integrated into the meaning and quality of life. There must be more and more and more success. The success-addicted person's relationships with others are extremely poor and lacking in depth. The primary relationship is with some*thing* rather than some*one*.

All of us need to feel a sense of success or accomplishment in life. Some experience little or none at all. The symbols of success are a problem. They are popularity, position, wealth, and power. Countless

numbers of people, however, experience a meaningful sense of accomplishment and success in life without ever having any of those symbols of success. But
as we reflect on success, many of us can identify with
something within ourselves that is akin to what exists within the person who becomes addicted to success. Those who seem to move in exactly the opposite
direction are indeed involved in the other side of the
same reality.

It is interesting to note here that the Bible speaks
of service not success. When success dominates life,
one is not free to be the servant of others.

Work Addiction

Work addiction usually accompanies success addiction, although it can be present by itself. It is common among corporation executives, physicians, and
clergy, but it can be found in almost any walk of life.
Some experience a special reward from work far beyond what most people get. Again we don't know
why. It provides a wonderful escape from and a sense
of healing for the common human dilemma.

Many people work hard and put in long hours without work becoming the controlling force in their lives.
They can let go of it, and they do. They can have fun
and relax without having to be involved in work.
They can enjoy being with spouse and family without
being preoccupied with work. Their life has balance
and quality relationships.

That is not true for the work addict. Separated
from work, like nonrecovering alcoholics separated

from drinking, work addicts get uptight. That's one of the reasons why some work addicts tie vacations in with work, if vacations are taken at all. Some consider sleep an undesired necessity.

Since this addiction is common among clergy, let's look at a few examples. The congregation and community in a variety of ways communicate that the excellent pastor is always available for anyone at anytime and is constantly busy. That can also be the message inside the pastor.

One Mother's Day early in my ministry I preached a sermon about the family being a gift of God. I thought it was a good sermon. Without really letting myself know it, I was hoping some of the members would think likewise and say so on their way out of church. Some did.

When we sat down to eat our noon meal with our two young sons, there was no expression on my wife's face to indicate that she thought it was a good sermon. In fact, the look on her face was negative. Her silence was loud. I didn't really let myself know it then, but that look of hers and that silence angered me.

It was five years later while listening to Dr. Bradley lecture on work addiction, that the light went on. By the expression on her face my wife had been saying, "If what you said in the pulpit this morning is true, how come we never see you?" And I had a rationalization an alcoholic could never use, not expressed verbally, but alive and well within myself: "I am doing all this work for the Lord's sake!"

The pain from the irony of it all has long been gone, and now remembrance brings with it a smile. Such an effort to escape from and attempt to heal the human dilemma isn't the answer. Fortunately, I hadn't yet succumbed to work addiction. Awareness and desire enabled me to change without outside help. But that light going on helped me identify something akin to the experience of the alcoholic, and I understood how work addiction can happen.

Another pastor sat beside his wife while she told the story of his work addiction without knowing what she was describing. One evening the pastor received a phone call during dinner. He immediately left the table to go see the person who had called. His wife reported, "Then our daughter said, 'Mother, maybe if I get sick dad would spend some time with me.'"

When the pastor heard his wife tell this story, he couldn't see that what she was talking about was a problem. He literally couldn't hear what she was saying. Like most work addicts, he was not free to assess whether people really needed to see him right then. Like alcoholism, work addiction is compulsive, repetitive, stereotyped behavior. The person is locked in and dominated by work. A person works long hours every day, taking only one day off in a whole year. The person has no awareness that work has had control for a long time.

Work addicts usually take vacations that can be tied in with work in some way. If they don't, the vacation usually consists of being on the go all the time to handle a high degree of restlessness and anxiety similar to the alcoholic in a nondrinking situation. There are no quality relationships on vacation either

Return to work brings a significant change. Back in the groove the person feels "oh so good," better than anything else the person can imagine.

Some on the way to alcoholism see that their drinking is not the answer. They change their behavior and life-style, getting help if necessary. Some will not end up with alcoholism. So, it is with success and work. Some people are on the way to addiction, but the chances of them seeing it are less, because the rewards enable them to continue living with the delusion that they have life. (By contrast, the predictable deterioration of life that comes with a progressive drinking problem can break up that delusion.) When the success or work addict has a heart attack or serious health problem and hears from the physician that he needs to slow down and learn to take it easy, he is no more able to change than an alcoholic who is told that he needs to cut down on his drinking. When threatened with divorce unless there is a change, there may be a promise to change, but change will not occur unless outside help is received.

Addiction to Sex, Money, and Pleasure

Another type of addiction has to do with sex and sexuality. In the past our society had an excessive amount of moralism and taboos about sex. Then not only did there come a new freedom, but freedom became license with no sense of moral responsibility. Sex was seen as a "thing" or "experience" by itself, apart from mutual love. Sex was perceived as being "it," the center and essence of life. And in that perception the individual was to get morally freed up to have "life." (Fortunately, that idea is becoming less popular.)

Still many today seek through sex an escape from and healing for their pain and brokenness. Some become addicted. But sex for its own sake proves to be an inadequate, disappointing, and hurtful escape — both for the individual and for his or her relationships. And this addiction to sex becomes tragically humorous, even silly, as people grow older. Sex can become a very deceptive god.

And how many people get hooked on money? Get more and save it. Or the more you have and the more you can spend, the happier you will be. Even many who don't have much of it, believe that money is really it. They dream of winning the lottery, or they read about the 10 wealthiest people in the country and think that that is "really it." They believe that money will remove, shield, or provide escape from pain, brokenness, and human limitation. They fall into the trap of thinking that the more money you have, the more you will have of life. Most of the truly financially poor in life know that that is a delusional hope for them. But at any financial level above that, such thinking can both be perceived overtly and subtly as the answer for healing and meaning. For many to be a success means to have money, and that is synonymous with having life. Persons from all economic levels get addicted to money, but money can never bring meaning within the common human dilemma. How true it is that you can't take it with you.

Pleasure, however it is perceived and experienced, can also be seen as the essence of life in the midst of life's pain, brokenness, and limitation. The more pleasure you can experience, the more you have life itself.

Sex, money, and pleasure are special gifts for enjoyment and sharing that can indeed enhance life and living in this world. But they are not life. They cannot provide healing, ultimate meaning, or lasting hope.

Food Addiction

Food addiction is a major health problem. In its severest form, the lying, the cheating, and the sneaking that goes with this addiction mimics alcoholic behavior and produces guilt, shame, and anxiety, which in turn triggers the desire for more food. The food addict loses control over his or her eating. Many of us can identify with this because of the common experience of being overweight and the difficulty of losing weight and maintaining the weight loss. And we do have to eat. What many people experience is that the excessive food intake increases their sense of well-being, because it reduces the anxiety and pain of our brokenness and limitation. Food, success, and work addiction are much tougher to treat and to recover from than alcohol addiction.

Addiction to Unhealthy Religion

There is also addiction to an unhealthy religion that is essentially moralistic while proclaiming the message of God's love. This religion exhibits the same kind of moralistic prejudice and judgmental, condemning attitudes that Jesus faced in the Pharisees. That was the only group Jesus came down hard on. He never responded in that way to people who were experiencing the pain of their brokenness and limitation. The people whose religion is marked by condemning and judging others think that they themselves are whole. They are unaware of their own brokenness and limitation. Through their religious experience they perceive themselves as the "righteous ones," who can clearly identify the "unrighteous ones." They are no longer in touch with the reality and pain of their own human condition. Of all the addictions, this addiction appears to be the "great deception," the most treacherous one. Seldom do any find the way back to the reality of their basic human condition.

Accepting Pain, Brokenness, and Limitation

Through our denial, rationalization, and blaming we seek to deny, escape from, and heal our pain, brokenness, and limitation. Anything that can positively change how we feel about ourselves, anything that can briefly reduce or remove our pain and anxiety can become addicting. In the process we can deceive ourselves into believing that we have escaped from, have control over, or have found healing for our pain. We can be led into the self-delusion that prevents healing, growth, and meaning.

Pain, brokenness, and human limitation are part of our common human condition. We all respond to this reality with the kinds of behaviors just described. We all need the awareness, understanding, and acceptance shown in a story told by an elderly pastor. In assessing his ministry he divided it into three phases. In the first phase he saw himself on the bank of the river. The people were in the river, and he was telling them how to get up on the bank where he was. In the second phase of his ministry he was on the bank reaching out to help the people get up on the bank where he was. In the third phase he had come to wisdom and understanding when he realized that he was in the river with the people. They were holding each other up, and underneath them all were the everlasting arms of God. In my journey I have learned that if there is to be any healing, hope, and meaning in life, there must come the awareness and acceptance that in our pain, brokenness, and human limitation, we are all in the river together. As we support each other and bear one another's pain, brokenness, and human limitation, underneath us all are the everlasting arms of God.

If that seems too far out in front of where you are in your journey in life, or if it seems too idealistic or sentimental or religious, I hope you will decide to continue on this journey for yet a little while.

CHAPTER THREE

The Omnipotent, Egocentric Self

From infancy on we have deep within us three delusional assumptions that continue on our journey into adulthood and throughout life. They get expressed in our attitudes, feelings, and behaviors. The expressions can be overt but more often are subtle and deceptive.

The three assumptions are: (1) I am in control or ought to be in control of all that has to do with my life; (2) I am at the center of the universe; (3) Everything and everyone ought to be spinning around me so I can have what I want and life will be the way I want it to be. These are infantile, to be sure, but they are common human assumptions. These inner assumptions not only cause us great difficulty in early childhood, but are in fact the great enemy within in regard to the reality of our pain, brokenness, and human limitation.

They are more than assumptions, they are expectations. There is that "inner king" demanding that life for me be that way. It is a matter of wanting *to do* it my way, but more than that, it is wanting it *to be* my way.

Understanding Surrender

Dr. Harry Tiebout, a psychiatrist, made a great contribution in helping us understand some of the basic problems and dynamics related to recovery from alcoholism as it relates to these three basic inner traits or forces. More than that, he provided some keen clinical insights into the nature of the human condition. He focused on "a sense of omnipotence" and egocentricity that are the essence of these three traits.

His understandings came from taking his alcoholism patients very seriously as human beings. He stayed close to them and listened carefully to what they were saying to him. If what they were saying didn't mesh with his psychiatric concepts and practice, he still took seriously what they were saying and exhibiting in their behavior.

Having applied all of his analytic concepts, approaches, and experience to his treatment of alcoholism patients, he completely failed to help them recover. He could have responded by saying that they really didn't want to quit drinking and get well, but he didn't do that, because he was convinced that many of them did want to quit drinking and get well. Rather, he decided that there was something he didn't yet understand. So, in the midst of his failure, he decided to stay with them.

As he was staying with them, one of his patients quit drinking and began to recover. Not only had she quit drinking, but there was clinical evidence of a basic inner change, which was reflected in her attitudes and behavior. Since he didn't have an explanation for this, he asked the patient if she would help him understand what had happened. She said that she had "surrendered." That was not a concept in his psychiatric practice, but he took her seriously. He decided that whatever she meant in that word "surrender" that was what he needed to better understand.

He asked the patient to write how she felt before and after this phenomenon that she called surrender. What she wrote was exactly what he had observed:

Before I felt . . .	*After I feel . . .*
unstable	at peace
tense	safe
nervous	composed
afraid	relaxed
guilty	contented
ashamed	thankful
pushed	cleansed
incapable	sane
uncertain	receptive
unworthy	prayerful
dismayed	

She added that she had now learned the meaning of humility and meditation. She didn't say that she felt all her problems were gone, as is often claimed in other conversion experiences. And there was no self-righteous attitude or rigid, stereotyped, repetitive, moralistic behavior that is often present in other conversion experiences. She knew she still had many of the problems of the "before state," but now there was something that was also "new." The something new felt good, and it gave her hope for a new life. As Dr. Tiebout sought to understand, he identified two inner realities that had been changed: one was *the sense of omnipotence* and the other was *egocentricity.* He identified these as infantile traits that are there at the start of life.

As he looked at all the traits he had seen in the patients with alcoholism, he identified three that were involved in surrender. He says, "At the start of life the psyche: (1) assumes its own omnipotence, (2) cannot accept frustration, (3) functions at a tempo allegretto with a good deal of staccato and vivace thrown in." The third trait he identifies also with the descriptive phrase "sense of hurry" or, as clearly evident in the infant and child, the expectation that there will be immediate satisfaction of need and desire.

"His Majesty, the Baby"

We tend to assume, falsely, that as we grow older we automatically grow up. Instead, the sense of omnipotence and egocentricity of infancy, which Dr. Tiebout refers to as "his majesty the baby," remains deeply embedded, often well-disguised, and functions with a good deal of self-deception.

It is possible to be an adult and yet have an internal emotional life in which the omnipotent ego is sitting on the throne with all the demands of the infant. It is possible to be an adult and be emotionally a young child or teenager. No adult ever reaches the full maturity of personhood, emptied totally of omnipotence and egocentricity. According to Dr. Tiebout, even underneath the feelings of inadequacy and inferiority is the infantile omnipotent ego clothed in self-deception.

There is that within us that tenaciously wants to remain on the throne of our lives, our sense of omnipotence and egocentricity. In our words, attitudes, feelings, and behaviors we can hear the infant, "his majesty the baby," inside sometimes shouting, "I want it my way. I want what I want. I want to be in control of all that has to do with my life, and I will prove that I am." We hear that inner reality shouting or saying through the quietness of self-pity, "I want what I want and I want it now." We hear that inner reality loudly and dramatically finding expression in impatience and low frustration tolerance. We hear it in the "why me?" and in the feeling "I am no good," or "I am nobody," or "nobody could love me," or "God could never love and forgive me." The person who makes those last statements has experienced a good deal of hurt and damage, and it will take a lot of caring and helping for the person to see the disguised reality that is really saying, "I am different, unique, and special." It's an inner perception and response that keeps the focus on me and keeps me at the center. It even includes the delusion that I have the power to change the nature of God.

How hard it is for any of us to recognize this hidden reality within us and to accept it—or to "surrender," as the woman said to Dr. Tiebout. Many people remain ignorant of this inner reality and the unconscious drives related to it that dominate their lives and push them around. As Tiebout said, "The inner king lies deep below the surface, far out of sight."

Dr. Tiebout said that the omnipotent ego, the inner king, never assumes that it should be stopped, can be stopped, or will be stopped. Think of the frustration level in crowded, slow traffic or any kind of delay that gets some people upset all of the time and others some of the time. Think of how difficult it is to accept the blockage that comes with the denial of our desires and plans or through illness or temporary disability. If you are a believer, think of how difficult it is to be still and know that God is God.

None of us, not even those raised within a healthy home, naturally gets freed up from that inner king or naturally descends from that imaginary throne. The only way this delusioned reality is altered is by what my colleague Jim McInerney called "a sufficient degree of pain." And for some, no degree of emotional or spiritual pain or no amount of blockage seems sufficient to crack the delusion. Some people are born, live, and die with it fully entrenched and dominating.

Some cannot imagine a life in which the omnipotent ego has surrendered. They see it as having no zip or drive or accomplishment or personal payoff. They say it can't work, and it is only an idealized delusion for life in our world. However, Dr. Tiebout says, "Life without Ego [in the sense in which it is here presented] is no new conception. Two thousand years ago Christ preached the necessity of losing one's life in order to find it." He also says that Freud could not conceive of life without that Ego (for him the original narcissism of the infant), and therefore he was never able to solve the riddle. Freud thought in terms of *reducing* that Ego, but never of *surrender*.

Tiebout came to the conclusion that when the patient said, "I surrendered," she was saying that something happened to that delusional, self-deceiving, infantile, omnipotent inner king entrenched in her being. And whatever happened freed her from its domination, opened up a new way of perceiving life, and provided an opportunity to have some positive attitudes and feelings and to learn a new way of life without the domination of the infantile inner king. Surrender opened the door to emotional and spiritual growth.

We all want to be in full control of our lives and destinies. We also want to control others and even the universe. We may not overtly show all this. It would appear too infantile, unreasonable, even ridiculous. Everybody knows at the intellectual level that it just isn't possible to have that kind of power and control, and it would sound too grandiose. But when you look at inner attitudes and feelings it is there. We get upset at ourselves when something in our behavior continues, even though we have decided to change it or get rid of it. We think we ought to be able to have more control. Or we may blame our behavior on someone else, which, among other things, means we want to control the other person. We can get angry when some decision is made that isn't to our liking over which we have no control or if a terrible accident or fatality comes into our lives. We want to be able to control and thus prevent such happenings. We, in fact, want to control God, because if we were God we would make sure such things didn't happen. Or we decide there is no God, because if we were God such things certainly wouldn't happen; they would be under our absolute control.

We not only want to exercise omnipotent control, but we expect that life ought to be and go our way. Within Dr. Tiebout's language, "his majesty the baby" is always there in a powerful and often dominating way.

These powerful and entrenched realities in our being do not want to accept pain, brokenness, or limitation. Observe how difficult it is for the infant to begin to hear that there are such realities. The first no's are never heard. The expectation is that "I will have what I want and have it when I want it," or "I will do what I want and do it when I want to." For the child to reach the stage where the reality of human limitation is heard is a major undertaking. And once it is heard, the child is still unwilling to accept pain, imperfection, and limitation. These inner traits continue into adult life.

There is no evidence that anyone naturally lets go of wanting life to be "the way I want it to be." Although life proves that we aren't omnipotent, it demonstrates that we want to be. In whatever areas there is any delusionary indication that we can be, we want that kind of control. Warm and loving parental relationships with needed and appropriate limit setting and discipline can assist in some movement towards growing up and letting go of the gross infantile behavior. But such relationships don't have the capacity of removing the assumptions and expectations of the "inner king."

Always within us is that which does not want to accept the realities of pain, brokenness, and limitation, that which wants to deny them, control them, escape from them, fix them, eliminate them. The sense of omnipotence and the egocentricity play a powerful and demanding role in relationship to the realities of our common human dilemma.

A Biblical Understanding of Human Nature

The Bible contends that these traits are a basic part of our human nature and dominate our inner being. It makes clear, as does Dr. Tiebout from his clinical insights, that they are with us at birth. They are not learned traits. What Dr. Tiebout describes as the sense of omnipotence and egocentricity makes up a big part of what is called human *sin* or our *sinful condition*. (If you have trouble with the word *sin,* don't let it throw you. For now, think of it as another word for the clinical realities of omnipotence and egocentricity within us.)

In the Garden of Eden story the Bible tells of Adam and Eve listening to the temptation, "You will be like God," which suggests, "You will have something even better and more of what you want." The Bible says that something needs to be done about the omnipotence and egocentricity within us. And it says that what needs to be done about that part of our being, we can't do. It is beyond our capability. We are ensnarled and lost in our omnipotence and egocentricity. We are sitting on the throne of our own lives as puppet gods. According to the Bible, there is no reality in that perception and desire, no hope in that delusion and bondage. No lasting fulfillment and meaning can be found in that way of life. None of us is God; the clear fact of life is that we live with pain, brokenness, and human limitation.

We need to be removed from the delusionary throne, to let go of wanting life to be egocentric. We need to be freed from all of that so we can join the human race in the reality of our pain, brokenness, and limitation. These infantile traits, this human sin, will always be there, but they need to lose their dominance and control of our lives. The questions in the Bible are, "How shall we be delivered? Who will deliver us from the captivity of this delusion and desire? What is the way, the truth, and the life for us in the reality of our pain, brokenness, and limitation?"

A psychiatrist who took his patients seriously and therefore listened to what they were really saying, feeling, and experiencing, identified the same human condition and problem that the Bible speaks of, but with a different language. With his language and understanding of omnipotent ego, inner king, "his majesty, the baby", and egocentricity, Dr. Tiebout provides a clearer understanding of the biblical description of the human condition as *sinfulness*. The church needs this clinical understanding from psychiatry and psychology to enhance the communication and understanding of the basic message of the Bible concerning our nature and condition. Years ago Dr. Albert Outler of the Perkins School of Theology said that the church will never have an adequate doctrine of humanity without the insights of psychiatry. The message of the Bible concerning our condition doesn't need the clinical validation of a psychiatrist or psychiatry, but Dr. Tiebout has provided that. It is also my conviction that psychiatry needs these clinical and spiritual understandings.

CHAPTER FOUR

Letting Go of the I, Me, Mine

Although I was raised within the Christian church, the word *surrender* was not a good word for me during the first 31 years of my life and the first eight years of my ministry. It suggested the tent-revival conversion, the instantaneous dramatic experience that resulted in a person seeing himself or herself as having been totally unrighteous and now totally righteous, an experience that resulted in a self-righteous, moralistic, judgmental way of life under the banner of Christian faith. All that was inconsistent with the gospel as I understood it.

In my journey, the word *surrender* took on a different content and meaning for me. It became a good, meaningful, and essential word that speaks to a profound need within the human condition.

Apart from this new understanding of the religious, spiritual, and clinical meaning, surrender generally is not perceived as being positive. Surrender carries the connotation of weakness and shame. But in our paradigm of alcoholism, surrender is seen as a human necessity and a positive evidence of strength. What Dr. Tiebout's patient was talking about when she used that word *surrender* both saved her life and changed it.

Dr. Tiebout believed that what had been profoundly changed in what she called *surrender* was that inner sense of omnipotence, that omnipotent ego. She accepted the reality of powerlessness and human limitation, her powerlessness over alcohol and an unmanageable life. Try as she might, she could not control or stop her drinking. Her delusion of omnipotence was shattered. Its dominating strength was diminished. The omnipotent ego had been dethroned. She was able to accept her powerlessness and her need to receive help outside herself. She found that help in Alcoholics Anonymous and in coming to believe in a power greater than herself.

Surrender meant she was able to consciously and unconsciously accept the fact that she was powerless. Surrender meant that she could consciously and unconsciously accept the reality of her human limitation. She was able to quit fighting the pain, the brokenness, the human limitation of her alcoholism, and to give in and accept it.

There is something that looks like surrender, but isn't. Dr. Tiebout called it *compliance*—which he described as half-hearted acceptance, submission, resignation, yielding, acknowledgement, and concession. With each of these words there is a feeling of reservation, a tug in the direction of nonacceptance. In A.A. the alcoholic who continues to drink is asked, "You have admitted powerlessness, but have you accepted it?" *Compliance* is conscious (intellectual) assent but unconscious (gut-level) non-acceptance. In compliance, the "omnipotent ego" has been weakened, but not dislodged from the throne.

The Process of Surrender

What brings about the intellectual and gut-level acceptance that is surrender? A certain degree of emotional and spiritual pain is required, which our paradigm of alcoholism readily provides.

A certain timing is also involved. Surrender is a process, not an event. Moving from denial to compliance to surrender, like all human change, is a process. For some, no matter how great the pain and whatever the timing and for whatever other reasons, surrender never comes.

Those in A.A. who do come to such surrender and recovery consistently say that something happened within them that they didn't make happen. They say it happened "by the grace of God." (If that phrase gives you problems, don't let it stop you on this journey at this point. For some that phrase has no particular religious association, but they are saying that something happened that they didn't make happen, and that is clinically observable.) They also say they are grateful to a higher power or to God for their surrender, without which they never would have recovered.

We have also learned that treatment staff can't make this surrender happen in alcoholic patients or their families. But we have learned that some things can enhance the possibility that surrender will occur.

By providing understanding and acceptance of alcoholism as an illness and the alcoholic as a person, and by employer and family confronting the alcoholic with the reality of the alcoholism, the possibility of surrender increases from 20% to 80%. That's dramatic. But it remains clear that humans can't make surrender happen. It is not a conscious decision or action.

Some nonalcoholism clinicians say that surrender sounds magical. It is not magical. It is clinically observable in hundreds of thousands of recovering people. It is not magical, but there is something *spiritual* in it.

Surrender cannot happen without the involvement of the person and the involvement with other people. The alcoholic needs to be involved in relationships that include listening, communicating, learning, and relating to others. There needs to be an internal desire or readiness to let go, to quit fighting, and to give in both within the conscious and unconscious, within the intellect and within the guts of the person.

Dr. Tiebout writes about the "unstoppable omnipotent" within, which never assumes that it will be stopped, can be stopped, or should be stopped. It remains a potentially dominating and destructive force. When that reality reassumes dominance in the alcoholic, the alcoholic becomes very distressed and usually returns to drinking, in the delusional belief of the omnipotent ego that "I can handle it." Herein lies the value of A.A., in which the person learns a new way of life. Included in that way of life is not only surrendering to and accepting human powerlessness over alcohol, but also learning to live with that reality "one day at a time." At the beginning of each day proper respect needs to be paid to the continuing internal "unstoppable omnipotent." The day is begun by asking for help, and the day is ended with an expression of gratitude.

Many stories could be told about alcoholics who experienced surrender and found a new way of life within their pain, brokenness, and human limitation. One day an alcoholic walked into my office without an appointment. He was obviously extremely anxious. He had been sober in A.A. for some months. He didn't want to drink, but he was a nervous wreck.

He said that they talked with him about "one day at a time." He said that there was no way in his condition that he could sustain that. Desperately he described what his drive home would be like. The four-lane highway he took to his home went by an abundance of bars. He would have to ask for help to get past each bar. If today was like the previous days, he would get home and not have had a drink, but he would be just as miserable as he was now. He knew that wasn't living, and he knew he didn't want to drink.

Some six or seven years later he called long distance about getting a friend admitted into treatment. He couldn't believe how well life was going for him. He still had problems, as other people do. But there had been no drinking. He did not recount all the help he had sought within A.A. and outside the organization but he did recall that office visit, his terrible anxiety, and his inability to sustain on "one day at a time," having to break it down to even smaller segments. And then he said, "If anyone ever would have told me that someday it could be one day at a time in my life and I would feel the way I feel now, I would have told them they were crazy."

Surrender for Nonalcoholics

How do we who are not alcoholics understand the need for surrender in our lives? Think of realities within your life and in your relationships with other people that you can't change. Then think of the ways in which your attitudes, feelings (frustration, impatience, anger, self-pity) and behaviors not only say you want to change that which you can't change but also how you indeed do try to change that or those whom you are powerless to change. Then try to come up with one dramatic evidence that the inner omnipotent ego remains alive within you and seems unstoppable.

I share one event from my life. Usually I handle driving in heavy traffic well, but one day I didn't. I was passing, weaving in and out, getting behind a slower driver who shouldn't have been in that lane. There were backups at the stop lights. My ability to cope with frustration was very low, and the frustration being experienced very high. But I didn't see it that way. The problem was out there in those other drivers.

Then came the long backup caused by a freight train crossing the highway. And then another. While watching this freight train and smoldering with frustration, the light went on inside me. I broke into convulsive laughter. Here were freight cars assembled from all over the United States and Canada, and I had been reacting as if that train should not have been there just for me. Now that's omnipotence and egocentricity!

Just as surrender is a process over time, so is the loss of surrender and the reascendance of the omnipotent ego. After the light went on that day, I became aware that the omnipotent self had been actively dominating for some time in my marriage and at work, being much better hidden at work than at home, as is often the case. When I shared the story with my wife, she smiled. It was no surprise to her. For me, for her, and for all of us, the inner omnipotence will never disappear or forever lay dormant. In a variety of ways, overt or subtle, obviously manifested or deceptively disguised, the omnipotent will always assume its unstoppableness and its rightful place on the throne. Some of its evidences are low frustration tolerance, a sense of hurry coupled with impatience, seeing one's personal distress as being caused by other people or some other outside reality, self-pity, a lack of gratitude, withdrawal, a lack of meaning, and striving after the delusionary symbols of love, acceptance, fulfillment, and hope.

We cannot dislodge the omnipotent ego and egocentricity from the throne or the center of our lives by our own reasoning or power. And something does need to happen to that inner reality, if for no other reason than the fact that life indeed does have pain, brokenness, and limitation. There can be no coming to terms with those human realities and acceptance of them as long as the omnipotent ego and egocentricity are dominating our lives. It is clear that surrender is essential if one is to live in and with these realities of human existence. In many ways compliance seems to work, but it leaves an internal restlessness and striving that can never be adequately satisfied.

There are a variety of surrender experiences related to human loss or limitation. Some are within and some outside religion. Some within religion are not healthy. They leave the person rigid, moralistic, judgmental, and certain of God's will in all things. Those are not the marks of spiritual health or signs of maturity. Some surrender experiences outside religion are also not healthy. They are known clinically to be hysteric or flight from reality. Some surrender within and outside religion results in a fixation, in which surrender is seen as taking place only in a specific kind of environment with a specific language and stereotyped behaviors that serve as the "signs." As in all human realities there can be healthy and unhealthy surrender.

Surrender and Conversion

The Bible sees surrender as a common human need. It is essential in redemption and for having life and having it abundantly. The Bible also makes it clear that it is a human need we cannot meet by ourselves. The Bible often speaks of surrender as *conversion*. Jesus said it this way, "You must be born anew."

The word *conversion* and the phrase *born anew* are negative for many people outside the church and also within the church. For years they were also negative words for me, and I needed to describe the realities they referred to with different language. Dr. Tiebout's insights expressed in a nonreligious context were helpful. His clinical description of the surrender process has made it possible to fill the word *conversion* with some good meaning, devoid of moralistic perceptions and unhealthy religious experiences.

In the gospel the need for conversion (surrender) is not related only to certain specific realities such as alcoholism or the loss of a limb or terminal cancer or the sudden news of an accidental death. Conversion (surrender) is related to the total human condition of pain, brokenness, and human limitation, including the inner omnipotence and egocentricity dominating human existence. In the biblical view the occupant of the throne is a false god, a deceptive god of self in whom no life can be found. According to the Bible the desires and strivings of the omnipotent egocentric self are delusional and strip a person of any possibility of having life and having it abundantly. The Bible maintains that the human reality includes finiteness, the inability to attain perfection, invulnerability, or omnipotence. A human being is not God.

The Bible calls this human reality *sin*. That is the spiritual word for this human reality. It is important to underscore here that in the gospel the words *conversion* and *sin* don't relate to a certain moralistic list of sins. Rather, they relate to the spiritual condition of humans in our relationship with God, self, and others.

The Bible's message is that we cannot do for ourselves what needs to be done: we can't dislodge the inner omnipotent on the throne and the egocentric self. We can't save ourselves from our human dilemma. From the human perspective, it is a hopeless situation. To live in a life that includes pain, brokenness, and human limitation dominated by omnipotence and egocentricity is not life and can lead to no basic fulfillment in life. It is to follow delusionary escapes and grasp for whatever one perceives as that which will enable a person to say, "This is it; this is life."

The message of the gospel is that God *is,* that he is our God and has created human life. God has acted on our behalf in history, beginning with Abraham and choosing the nation of Israel as the people through whom he would provide our deliverance, enable conversion within, and make it possible for us to have life in him with meaning, satisfaction, gratitude, hope, and eternal promise in the midst of our pain, brokenness, and human limitation. The biblical message is that such a life can become a human reality. We indeed can be born anew by the grace of God.

The gospel includes the strange, haunting, story of a God active in history, who in the fullness of time became human, born of Mary, and lived among the people, entering into their pain, brokenness, and human limitation. His name is Jesus, which means "Savior," for he will save the people from their sinful condition. Because this is so unbelievable and so incomprehensible, the Bible calls it "the foolishness of God." But it also says that in this event in history, in this person—his life, death, and resurrection—we can experience the power of God for salvation.

How can anyone believe this? We can't believe it by our own reasoning or power. Faith can only be accomplished by God's Spirit working within. Reason cannot achieve this faith, and our human omnipotence cannot accept the need for such a faith.

New Life—Day by Day

The mark of conversion in the Christian faith is the confession that "Jesus is Lord." That means that there is a new occupant on the throne. There is a new center other than self. Jesus becomes the Way, the Truth, and the Life for life and in death. In Jesus, God but also human, we see a human life of service to others, a person emptied of omnipotence and egocentricity, praying "Your will be done," giving thanks to the Father, and glorifying his name. Jesus said that this is life, abundant in the midst of the pain, brokenness, and human limitation. And this is what Paul meant when he said, "If anyone is in Christ, he is a new creation" (2 Cor. 5:17).

Even after her surrender Dr. Tiebout's patient talked about still having many problems. Here, too, it is important to underscore that in the conversion talked about by Jesus and in the letters of St. Paul, although there is something new, the old remains. Conversion does not result in the elimination of the omnipotent ego and egocentricity. In the language of the Bible, conversion does not result in the removal of our sin. Conversion does not make us perfect, but there is something new. The new is, "Christ is my Lord in life and death." He is at the center. There is a new desire expressed in a prayer, "Your kingdom come. Your will be done on earth as in heaven." But the new is not there perfectly or totally. After his conversion, Paul called the old the "flesh" and the new the "spirit" and describes realistically the battle that exists between "flesh" and the "spirit." It is clear from the Bible that after conversion the omnipotent ego and the egocentricity—sin—still remain. And at any time the omnipotence and egocentricity can again assume domination.

In our paradigm of A.A. the way of life includes "one day at a time." The Christian gospel includes the same awareness of a daily battle against omnipotence and egocentricity. Luther expressed it well in his Small Catechism: "Our sinful self . . . should be drowned through daily repentance; and that day after day a new self should arise," that the new person may live seeking to do the will of the Lord. The prayer that needs to arise daily from within is, "Your kingdom come. Your will be done." The desire of the old is to have it my way. The desire of the new that comes through conversion is that Christ the Lord will live within and through one's life.

In the Christian message Christ is revealed as being our higher power, our God who has come to redeem us and restore us to a new way of life in the midst of our pain, brokenness, and limitation. The way to this restoration and newness is the same as in our paradigm of A.A. It is the way of surrender or conversion. Both in the nonreligion paradigm of A.A. and in the Christian religion, there is this common basic spiritual human need of surrender. We can manufacture compliance by ourselves, but by ourselves we cannot create surrender. That is one of our most basic human limitations. The Bible says that we need God, and we need to let go and let God redeem us from our omnipotent, egocentric self.

CHAPTER FIVE

Letting Go of Moralism

In the early days of Alcoholics Anonymous religion and religious words were problematical. What people in A.A. had experienced in surrender and recovery was spiritual, but it was outside religion. As they began to put together their common experience and hope into words and sentences, which eventually were called the Twelve Steps, they did not want to become another religion or sound like a religion. For many of them religion was a negative. No religion or religionists had been able to offer them any real help or hope. All they had experienced in religion was moralism, judgment, and condemnation, which was felt as rejection. Back in the days when alcoholics were generally seen as the moral reprobates and outcasts in society, it was said that there were two groups alcoholics couldn't stand—police and preachers.

These early members of A.A. struggled to identify words that fit their common experience of belief in a power greater than themselves. This coming to believe in a power greater than themselves was for them the key reality in finding hope and strength in their surrender to pain, brokenness, and powerlessness. There was disagreement about how to refer to this power. The agnostics and atheists who had experienced this power outside themselves would not accept the word *God.* An Episcopalian minister's son wanted to use the name Jesus; they would have none of that. Finally, they agreed on "power greater than ourselves." Once they agreed on that, they apparently didn't have any major problems with including the word *God* in any of the rest of the Twelve Steps.

The Problem of Moralism

The problem with the word *God* and some of the other religious words had to do with moralism. That was the problem for these early members of A.A. working on the Twelve Steps. That has been the problem of people in all generations. So on this journey, before proceeding any further, we needed to address the nature and content of *moralism,* of being *moralistic.* The religious language that needs to be used in communicating and addressing our spiritual needs has to be emptied of moralism.

When I entered this specialized ministry in 1955, I was told, "It is important that as a pastor you are not moralistic in your relationships and communications with alcoholics. Alcoholics can't stand moralism, and that is what they have received and expect from the church and pastors." Soon after this I became acquainted with A.A.

In reading A.A. literature, attending A.A. meetings, and talking with recovering alcoholics in their fellowship, I saw that in their program alcoholics were presented very clearly with a moral or spiritual program for hope and recovery. It appeared that the Twelve Steps program contradicted the statement, "You can't be moralistic." Yet it was obvious that these people who had all kinds of problems with God, religion, and religious words didn't see any contradiction in their use of some of the religious moral language. What I came to see is that there is a difference between *moralism* and *morality,* between being *moralistic* and being *moral,* and that the difference is tremendous.

Moralism is not only an attitude but also a behavior. Moralism is conditional and judgmental. Moralism attaches strings to acceptance so it is in fact nonacceptance. Moralism is seeing oneself as being more righteous than another person. Moralism is not only the rejection of unacceptable behavior, such as the behavior of alcoholism, but it is rejection of the person in whose life the behavior exists.

Moralism is "shouldism": "You shouldn't be like that. You shouldn't do that. You shouldn't have done that. You shouldn't feel that way." Or, "I shouldn't be like that. I shouldn't do that. I shouldn't have done that. I shouldn't feel that way."

Although "shouldism" looks like evidence that the person wants to change negative realities in his or her life, the A.A. paradigm assures us that change won't happen. As long as alcoholics moralize or say "I *shouldn't* be an alcoholic," the drinking will continue. That is true with all human problems in which change is needed. Try to identify any basic negative reality in your life that was changed as a result of "shouldism." It is one of the best ways to assure no change.

This is because moralistic shouldism is nonacceptance. By contrast, seeing alcoholism as an *illness* helps in getting alcoholics to get off the shouldism that blocks acceptance of their human limitation.

When the shouldism goes and the person nonmoralistically can say, "This is me and my condition, and I want to change," the change can come. When surrender or acceptance comes, the moralistic shouldism dissipates. This is a reality we can observe in our personal living.

Moralism needs to have other people believing, thinking, feeling, talking, and behaving the way the moralist "thinks they should." Inherent in such a need is the preservation of its own self-delusion, self-justification, self-comfort, and self-security.

Moralism seeks and points to scapegoats. This behavior makes clear the irresponsibility of moralism. Moralism is blaming behavior. Blaming is part of scapegoating, but it is different, because it also involves self-blame. And we can be extremely moralistic with ourselves in self-blaming.

I was told, "You can't be moralistic with alcoholics." Moralism had been the response of society and the church, and alcoholics were being just as moralistic with themselves as everyone else. There was no hope in that because moralism communicated lack of understanding and mutual identification, together with judgment, condemnation, and rejection. Indeed the need to better understand the meaning of *moralistic* over against *moral, moralism* over against *morality* was an important, necessary learning for the church in developing its ministry to alcoholics and their families.

Moralism in the Church

The words *God, Jesus, Christian church, religion, sin,* and *belief* are filled with moralistic perceptions and content in many peoples' lives inside and outside the church, just as they were for the early members of A.A. Yet the gospel teaches that God revealed in Christ is not the great moralist. However, because the Christian church is made up of humans, and we all have moralism embedded within us, the perception and communication of the gospel's message of God's love toward us have often been distorted and contaminated with our moralism. The religious words and language of the Christian message need to be emptied of moralistic perception and content.

We learn much about moralism from the New Testament. Moralism is charging Christ with violating the rules of the Sabbath by feeding hungry people and healing the sick. Moralism is condemning Christ for associating with harlots and publicans. Moralism is the religious people within the community with stones in their hands to throw at the adulterous woman. Moralism is the Pharisee in the temple. Moralism is the brother who is angry and disillusioned when the father throws his arms around the returning brother and celebrates with a banquet. Moralism in the New Testament is the Pharisees with their own set of absolute rules that are believed and taught as God's certain will. Moralism, therefore, behaves as if it always knows what God's will is in everything. Moralism is unaware of its self-delusion of self-omniscience and self-righteousness. Believing that it knew both God and God's will, moralism wanted Christ crucified.

When the self-delusion of moralism becomes cloaked within the language of the gospel and God's grace, it is at best misperception and at worst demonic. Within the Christian church, moralism puts the Christian faith and life into its box of do's and don't's, its required belief systems, its circumscribed religious experiences, language, and behavior. Then you are either in or out. In this context the box not only is a symbol of being closed in and rigid; it also is a symbol of moralism's need to provide for itself the security such a self-made belief system requires.

Jesus' story about the son who leaves his father's home, squanders his life and inheritance, and then returns is an interesting one in terms of moralism. It is identified as the story of the prodigal son. Perhaps most of us in the church are more like the moralistic son remaining in the father's house than the prodigal son who left and returned. The son who remained with his father in his father's house never really knew his father. He had projected his moralism onto his image of his father. So when the non-moralistic father welcomed his brother back with open arms with a banquet and a celebration, the son who had remained in his father's house was confused, disillusioned, angry, and self-righteous.

Moralism in the church is separating the sheep from the goats, the righteous from the unrighteous, the saved from the unsaved. In so doing it usurps authority belonging only to God.

Jesus' response to moralists is shocking. "You are like whitewashed tombs which look fine on the outside but are full of dead men's bones and rotten stuff on the inside." Moralism is not of the mind and spirit of Christ. Theologically and clinically moralism is also naive and simplistic in its understanding of the nature of humans, the nature of sin, and the nature of human pain, brokenness, and limitation.

When people perceive the Christian message in terms of the conditional, judgmental, and condemning content of moralism, then religious words such as *God, Jesus, Christian religion, Christian faith, Christian life,* and *sin* are rejected.

Moralism in the Christian church causes God to be perceived as being conditional, judgmental, and condemning even while being presented as a loving God revealed in Christ. The Christian religion is seen as a message of how to try and come to terms with such a schizophrenic God. The word *sin* is seen as meaning a moralistic list of do's and don't's. Christ is seen as the great moralist. Faith is seen as having no real certain hope. And the Christian life is seen as taking all the freedom, fun, and enjoyment out of life.

Some people have left the church because of such distorted moralistic perceptions and beliefs. Others have become inactive, because they figure you can live such a perceived "moral" life outside as well as inside the church. Still others are held within the church and even attracted to the church because of such moralistic perceptions and beliefs. They find much comfort and security living within the moralistic box.

The Christian message says that such moralistic perceptions, attitudes, feelings, and behaviors are not just learned from others but are part of our sinful nature. It is a large part of our sin and contaminates our perception not only of God but also of our sin. Moralism is a dominant reality within us. It finds expression in our lives every day. It is not only embedded within us, but it is also something we tenaciously hold on to in our relationship with God, self, and others. It is something none of us can ever completely get rid of. Only in Christ do we see the purely nonmoralistic human life. There is no moralism in his being. *This is part of his essential uniqueness.*

In the gospel we are assured that by Christ's presence within us moralism can cease to dominate and control our lives, just as our omnipotence and egocentricity can cease to dominate our lives as the spirit of Christ finds expression. Moralism is something that Christ continually calls us to let go of, to be freed from in order that we might become more like him— the nonmoralistic one.

The phrase *higher power* got the people in A.A. out of the moralistic perception and experience; then they had no problem using words like *God, believe, moral, moral defects, God's will, prayer,* and *spiritual awakening.* Emptied of moralism, those are all good words that speak to the reality of the human condition and human need. If the members of A.A. as a nonreligious fellowship could so empty these words of moralism as a result of their spiritual experience, how much more so ought the fellowship of the Christian church be able to empty its religious words and language of moralism as a result of the faith and spiritual experience with Christ, in whom there is no moralism. One of the reasons the message is called the gospel—good news—is because there is no moralism in this news.

CHAPTER SIX

Grace without Moralism

We all have the basic human need to be understood, identified with, and accepted. In A.A. alcoholics find such a human environment around alcoholism. There is no feeling of moralistic judgment, condemnation, and rejection, only understanding, acceptance, and mutual identification. When recovering alcoholics within A.A. say, "by the grace of God," that accepting human environment is an essential part of the meaning of grace. For them it was an unexpected experience; it was what they needed to begin anew and continue. It was better than what alcohol could offer. It enabled and asked them to face the reality of their condition. It provided an opportunity for healing and newness. It provided hope and promised meaning. It felt so good because there was so much good in it. It made them feel grateful. That's the nature of the grace they experienced in the relationship with others within the fellowship.

Within that kind of human environment they came

to accept their powerlessness over alcohol, and they also came to believe in a power greater than themselves who could restore them to sanity. Within that fellowship of grace, they came to believe in a God who was graceful towards them as alcoholics, who met them in their human limitation, who was for them not against them, who would support them, give them strength, continue with them in their recovery—a God to whom they could commit their lives in their pain, brokenness, and human limitation.

A God Full of Grace

The word *grace* is an important word and reality for the human condition. It has significant meaning for our relationship with God, with our own self, and with one another. The Bible includes many revelations about God. One clear revelation in the promise, birth, life, teachings, suffering, death and resurrection of Christ is that God is full of grace. That means God is love and that God's love is total, unconditional, and freely given. God initiates movement towards us and takes benevolent action on our behalf. In the Christian message grace means that God freely enters into our human situation, lives among us, takes into his being our pain, brokenness, and limitation, and all the consequences of it. It means that he bears our burdens in his body and in his life. It means that he fully gives himself to us and for us. Grace means that he comes to be with us, to redeem us, to show himself as the way, the truth, the life—as our way, our truth, our life—and to enter into the human experience of death so that he overcomes the power of death for us. Grace means that God comes to us and reveals himself to us, because we can't by ourselves find him or come to know and believe in him as he really is.

To believe in the God revealed in Christ is to know that God is not dominated or controlled by the moralism that permeates our being. In the gospel he reveals himself as having no moralism but being full of grace. This statement does not imply that grace is only nonmoralism, but simply that there is no moralism in grace. The God revealed in the gospel is full of grace.

The gospel also makes it clear that for moralists such as us, the written word would not be sufficient to reveal God's grace. We need more than reading and hearing about it. That word needs to become incarnate, needs to become human, not only to do the work of our redemption, but also to show us in flesh and blood our God as a God who is full of grace. God's grace had to become the living Word among us—relating with people speaking, touching, healing, giving life. And as we through faith see God in human flesh, clearly he is full of grace and there is no moralism in him.

Even so, our lives, and the lives of all those who have called him Lord, declare that although this is all clear in Christ, it hasn't been that easy for us to see, believe, and live. Even with the opportunity to be personally with him, his first disciples were blocked by their own moralism from seeing, understanding, and believing in him as full of grace, unconditional in his love. Luther evidenced keen insight into the human condition when he said, "I believe that I cannot by my own understanding or effort believe in Jesus Christ my Lord, or come to him."

God's grace was revealed not only in the incarnation but also in the sending of the Holy Spirit. While yet on earth Christ promised the Holy Spirit would come to guide the disciples into this truth and empower them to believe. And so there is the rest of Luther's statement, "But the Holy Spirit has called me through the Gospel, enlightened me with his gifts, sanctified and kept me in true faith."

And before he left this earth Christ commanded his disciples to carry this message, this good news of God's grace towards us, to all the earth and when doing so to baptize in the name of the Father, Son, and Holy Spirit so the fullness of his grace could be received. Luther said that whenever doubts assailed him about God's grace he always returned to his Baptism.

Once the disciples by the power of the Holy Spirit came to see and believe the unconditionalness of God's love for us in Christ, they joyfully, confidently, and boldly became his witnesses. They began to turn the world upside down by proclaiming this message. And the world has never been the same since.

The Church and Grace

However, because the moralism within us is deeply embedded and can so easily assume a dominant position, the Christian church has always had difficulty with preaching, teaching, and being an expression of Christ and his grace. Moralism has been reflected in the history of the church, in our teachings about God and God's will, and in our relationships with our own selves and each other. In the most painful and limiting experiences of life in our brokenness, the answers so often sought and given within the church have been moralistic.

Think of how quickly the church went from the witness of grace by the disciples to the darkness of the Middle Ages. It seemed as if the light of the gospel indeed had been extinguished. Moralism was being communicated as the gospel. God's love and forgiveness were presented as something that needed to be and could be earned and even bought.

Then the light of grace broke through again in Reformation. However, even those who became a part of the Reformation began to distort and make conditional the grace of God in their theological statements and in their preaching and teaching. Besides the problem of our moralism, there has also been the problem of having difficulty understanding the difference between *moralism* and *morality*. That in turn has resulted in a major problem in understanding freedom and human responsibility as part of and in relationship to grace, and therefore the making of grace conditional.

After all this historic difficulty with grace there seems to be something new and hopeful. The profound significance of Pope John XXIII's election and his calling of Vatican Council II is just beginning to become apparent. There is another reformation going on within the church. Surely within that election and council there was clear evidence of grace being expressed. Teachings and traditions that did not reflect grace have been and are being modified and even eliminated. Ecumenism among Christian churches is evolving in new and positive ways.

As perhaps never before since the early church a climate exists for Christ's gracious spirit to be present and effective. Within the church we are hearing much more about mercy, justice, peace, caring for the poor and brokenhearted, feeding the hungry, and providing hope for those who have no hope. We are hearing more about carefully looking after the earth and the universe which are from and under God's grace. These are basic marks of the life and teachings of our gracious Lord. But because of the moralism within us and the nature of life's experiences, we need to hear it again and again and again in both Word and sacrament that our God revealed in Christ is full of grace.

The Cross of Grace

We still must ponder the seemingly impenetrable, unfathomable mystery of God's grace and God's righteousness and justice in Christ on the cross. His human suffering is understandable; other people also suffered pain and death by crucifixion. It was inevitable that moralism would need to kill him, particularly since he claimed to be God's Son and was living and preaching a message that God was full of grace. But within the message of the cross is the announcement that Christ paid the price for our sin; he did satisfaction for our sin; he fulfilled the righteousness and justice of God on our behalf. The need for the sacrifice of animals to satisfy the justice of God for sin in the Old Testament is carried on in the New Testament in the shedding of the blood of a human, God's Son, who takes into his being all of our sin, endures the consequences, and pays the price: "My God, my God, why have you forsaken me?"

There was a time in my life journey when I had no problems with the cross and this question of God's righteousness and justice. Now it seems more of a mystery, and I have some difficulty with the satisfaction of God's righteousness and justice being within his gracious redemptive activity for us. I do know that Jesus said the cross was necessary for our redemption, and on the cross, near the end of his life, he said, "It is finished." What needed to be done for us and our redemption by our gracious God has been completed.

Some have no problem with this. Some seek to explain away the righteousness and justice of God in the cross as being a misinterpretation or a contradiction of grace. Others try to provide intellectualized, rationalistic theological understanding of God's love and justice. On this journey I have ended up doing neither of these. I continue to live with the mystery, believing that within the cross is not only the love but also the righteousness and justice of God. In this life we do see through a glass dimly, we still have only partial understanding of God and his grace. But of this we are certain: he is full of grace, and he would have us live gracefully with him, with our individual selves, and with one another.

I learned something of God's grace from the non-religious fellowship of A.A. First of all, it became clear that God's gracious presence, help, and involvement with his people is not limited only to those who come to confess Christ as Lord, as is too frequently implied in some preaching and teaching within the church. Whenever, wherever, and in whatever manner a person experiences the personal reality and acceptance of human pain, brokenness, and limitation, God is present with grace and strength—whether or not the person is aware of it and whether or not a person believes in God in a particular way. Moralistic attitudes and doctrines within the church have provided considerable contamination and distortion of this truth.

Because of its environment of understanding, acceptance, and common identification—of grace—the A.A. fellowship is a paradigm for all of us. If alcoholics experience the need and meaning of grace in accepting human limitation, in experiencing healing, and finding a new life in the midst of their pain and brokenness within a fellowship like A.A., how much more ought we all to recognize that this is our common human need and seek to provide more of that kind of human environment for one another in our relationships together.

If this nonreligious fellowship is able to provide such a grace-full human environment for one another in the pain, brokenness, and human limitation of their alcoholism, how much more so ought we who confess faith in Christ our Lord who is full of grace be able to provide for ourselves and others this kind of human environment. If in this nonreligious fellowship these people are able to experience the grace of God by coming to believe in a "power greater than themselves," how much more ought we who confess faith in God revealed in Jesus Christ be able to experience the fullness of his grace for our whole life. Clearly the message in the gospel's revelation of our God is, "Grace be unto you and peace from God our Father and the Lord Jesus Christ."

CHAPTER SEVEN

Morality within Grace

In our paradigm of Alcoholics Anonymous, we have seen the absence of moralism about alcoholism and the experience of grace in understanding, acceptance, and mutual identification. There is also a *moral* way of life, *moral* steps that need to be taken. Here are the Twelve Steps of A.A.

1. We admitted we were powerless over alcohol—that our lives had become unmanageable.
2. Came to believe that a Power greater than ourselves could restore us to sanity.
3. Made a decision to turn our will and our lives over to the care of God as we understood Him.
4. Made a searching and fearless moral inventory of ourselves.
5. Admitted to God, to ourselves and to another human being the exact nature of our wrongs.
6. Were entirely ready to have God remove all these defects of character.

7. Humbly asked Him to remove our shortcomings.
8. Made a list of all persons we had harmed and became willing to make amends to them all.
9. Made direct amends to such people whenever possible except when to do so would injure them or others.
10. Continued to take personal inventory and when we were wrong, promptly admitted it.
11. Sought through prayer and meditation to improve our conscious contact with God as we understood Him, praying only for knowledge of His will for us and the power to carry that out.
12. Having had a spiritual awakening as a result of these steps, we tried to carry this message to alcoholics, and to practice these principles in all our affairs.

No Grace without Morality

A.A. helped me see not only that there is no moralism in grace, but that there is no grace without morality. Within the Christian message that statement leads into the historic question of God's law revealed in the Bible and God's grace revealed in Christ. If God's grace is indeed free and unconditional, how then can there be God's moral law, commandments, required obedience? How can law and gospel be together? It seems so contradictory; law and gospel seem mutually exclusive. Yet in Christ and in his teachings they are together. He who is grace lives a life fully in harmony with God's moral law. He is the obedient one who fulfills God's law—

on our behalf. When he thought about the cross, his sweat became as great drops of blood. He agonized. He prayed, "My Father, if it is possible, may this cup be taken from me. Yet not as I will, but as you will" (Matt. 26:39). And obediently he went to the cross. Later, to his disciples, he said, "Therefore go and make disciples of all nations, baptizing them in the name of the Father and of the Son and of the Holy Spirit, and teaching them to *obey* everything that I have commanded you" (Matt. 28:19-20).

How can we understand God's law as part of grace? In creating us in his image, God implanted in our being his moral law, which is the law of love. Without it, we cannot be persons created in the image of God. God's moral law of love is essential to personhood, to relationship with God, self, and others. In this sense, God's law must be fulfilled in order for our personhood and our relationships to be fulfilled. God's moral law is indeed grace, because it is essential to our being. Without it we would not be persons in relationship. If we were able to perfectly fulfill God's law, we would be able to perfectly fulfill personhood. God is love, and God's moral law is love. So it is that God's law is also God's grace for us.

What God says about the law for us is different from what the people in A.A. say about their moral steps. They say, "This is what we found we needed to do," or "This is how we found we needed to live." But our Lord says that he requires obedience to his law. To his disciples he said, "Teach them to obey." Anything less than obedience to the law of God is not good enough, is not sufficient for people created in his image. It is indeed the only way that we can have abundant life. So it is that in his grace, God promises to free us from the domination of sinful disobedience. We may live a life that prays, "Your will be done," a life that seeks to be obedient to his moral law of love. We were created for such obedience, for such a life. And we have been redeemed for such obedience, for such a life.

As parents teach us obedience, they may err. So as we grow into adulthood, we have to decide for ourselves what we will and will not believe and do that our parents taught us. If they taught us that God's love is conditional based on our obedience, we may come to realize that isn't true. If they taught us through attitudes expressed that God is a god of racism and that obedience is staying apart instead of living together, we may come to realize that isn't true. If they taught us that obedience doesn't mean worshiping regularly, we may come to realize that isn't true. If they taught us that obedience is giving a little of our money rather than giving generously, we may realize that isn't true. If they taught us that it is all right to ignore the poor and let them look after themselves, we may come to realize that isn't true. If they taught us we can abuse our bodies and God's earth through selfishness, pollution, and neglect, we may come to realize that isn't true. Parents may err.

God has not erred in his law. God's commandments are sure from generation to generation. The obedient life of Christ is the fulfillment of God's law, and in that obedience we see the fulfillment of personhood.

Part of our sinful nature is that we want to establish our own law. None of us wants to be told how to live, and today we have seen a significant weakening of the concept of obedience. "No one can tell me what to do! I have my human rights!" people declare. Christ makes it clear that there can be no human rights, no human fulfillment, without human obedience to God's moral law of love for God, self, and others.

But people say, "You can't command love." The fact is, Jesus does. He alone can do that. As the God full of grace he can do no other. Without it persons can live, but they can't have abundant life. In this sense God's law is our life, and as such it is inherent in grace.

Law and Gospel

The historic law-and-gospel theology is expressed in the statement that God's law convicts us of our sin and the gospel proclaims the assurance of grace and redemption. Given what has just been said about God's law being grace, this law-and-gospel theology needs to be revised. The law is not separate from the gospel or grace. The law is "within the gospel," "within grace"; the law is part grace.

Just as the Word had to become incarnate, not only to accomplish our redemption but to show us in flesh and blood the God full of grace, so the fulfillment of the law had to become incarnate, not only for our redemption, but also so that we could see the true nature of the law and the true fulfillment of the law in the flesh and blood life of Jesus. Without the law incarnated in him we cannot understand God's moral law. Just as Jesus is the New Testament revelation

of God's grace, so is he also the New Testament revelation of God's law and the fulfillment of that law.
He is the embodiment of grace and the embodiment
of the law.

He said that he does not remove the law given to
Moses but that he makes the law new. That newness
could only come in and through the Incarnation. That
newness was revealed in his trust of the Father's
love, in his love for the Father, in his commitment
to the Father's will. That newness was revealed in
his breaking of the moralistic law of the Sabbath to
be obedient to God's law of love by feeding the hungry
and healing the sick. It was there in his being present
unconditionally with the publicans and sinners, the
adulterous woman, the Samaritan, the despised tax
collector, the sick, the lame, the blind, the diseased
outcasts. It was there in his story about the father
who threw his arms around his returning son and
had a banquet. It was there in his statement, "Into
your hands I commit my spirit." But moralism
couldn't hear it, see it, understand it, or comprehend
it. In Jesus' life, God's nonmoralistic moral law of
love is revealed and fulfilled. The law is not separate
and apart from the gospel, from grace. The law is
"within the gospel," "within grace."

Only as the law is "within grace," in the personhood and life of Jesus, can it truly convict us of our
sin, brokenness, and human limitation. In the New
Testament there is, therefore, no understanding of
God's moral law and conviction of sin except in and
through Jesus. Jesus is the law of God and the grace
of God.

For any violations of God's moral law of love a price is paid, but not in the way of moralism, with its conditional, judgmental, condemning perception of God. Rather, the violations of God's moral law of love always damage self and others. In this sense, the judgment of God is built into his creation.

Within a family and in relationship to oneself, the results of the violation of the law of love are both inevitable and discernible. We need only think of the price paid when hurting family members are moralistic with each other and when an individual family member moralizes with himself or herself. The estrangement and rejection that are felt, the pain, and the lack of self-esteem experienced, the going nowhere in growth and newness in life make up an extremely costly price.

This is also true for society. One example is the price that we have paid for violations of God's moral law of love toward black people—the riots and burnings. These riots happened because blacks are humans created in the image of God but violated through the failure of whites to be obedient to God's moral law of love. For such violation a price will inevitably be paid. So it is now and will continue in South Africa until blacks are free and considered equal.

And so it is that with violations of God's law, guilt is both real and necessary—real because of the violations of God's moral law of love, and necessary for repentance, renewal, and growth. The grace of God—his unconditional love—makes possible the ongoing experience of forgiveness and release from guilt towards greater fulfillment in obedient love. Christ makes it clear that there can be no human rights and no human growth or fulfillment without human obedience to God's moral law of love.

So when people say that you can't command love, the fact is that God did and God does. God is the only one who can do it, and God does it. And so it is that Jesus says, "Teach them to obey all that I have commanded you." Without such obedience, people can live, but they can't have abundant life. In this sense God's commandment, God's moral law of love, is our life and as such is inherent in grace as revealed in Jesus Christ.

Christ—the Fulfillment of God's Law

So essential is God's moral law of love, the need for obedience in order to have life and fulfillment, and the inevitable price to be paid for violations of the law towards God, self, and others, that for our sake God became human, God sent Jesus to redeem us from our disobedience. He showed us life as the fulfillment of God's moral law of love. He became the fulfillment of God's law for us. He took into his being all our violations of God's law of love and paid the inherent price of all our violations. (This thought needs to be pursued more in regard to what has been referred to in the previous chapter as the "seemingly impenetrable, unfathomable mystery of God's grace and God's righteousness and justice in the Cross.) He became the obedient one, obedient unto death, even the death on the cross. Thus it is that the God full of grace became our *obedient* God.

In our paradigm, if alcoholics violate the moral steps of A.A., if omnipotent ego, egocentricity, and wanting it their own way assume control again, they usually get drunk and at best are extremely miserable. The new life they had found is gone. They have lost their lives again. There is no meaning, hope, or fulfillment.

So it is with God's law of love within us as a gift of grace. When self takes over, wanting life to be "my way," we are moving away from life. We are losing our life. Only as Christ's spirit is alive within, so that we are seeking obedience to and fulfillment of his moral law of love, can we have and experience meaning, hope, and fulfillment. The nonreligious paradigm of A.A. helped me better understand that grace is free but not cheap, as Bonhoeffer has written. The paradigm helped me better understand that there is no grace of God without the morality of God. It helped me better understand that without the gracious gift of God's moral law interpreted and lived out in the life of Christ, we are indeed lost in seeking the nature and fulfillment of life as people created in the image of God. On this journey, I learned that there is no moralism in grace and morality, and there is no grace without morality—the morality of God's law of love fulfilled in Christ.

CHAPTER EIGHT

Morality, Human Responsibility, and Grace

Moralism has not only obscured the understanding of *grace;* it has also obscured the understanding of *morality.*

Like moralism, morality is behavior, including the behavior of believing that the God revealed in Jesus Christ is our Savior full of grace. Speaking of the *behavior of faith* implies that such faith is alive within a person and finding expression in life. This is what is meant by, "The kingdom of heaven is within you." If it is there, it is there in the behavior of faith.

Morality in the Christian Faith

So morality in the Christian faith is the behavior of believing in a God full of grace and believing that only a God of unconditional love can be our Savior. Morality is the behavior of believing that there is no life and no hope in a God who is moralistic, conditional, and condemning. Faith is more than "knowing about"; it is believing and accepting and living the reality of the revealed grace of God in Jesus Christ.

When unconditional acceptance is accepted unconditionally through faith in Jesus Christ, that is morality. Morality is inseparable from faith in the God full of grace. Morality is also gut-level acceptance of one's own sinful being within a nonmoralistic context. In fact, believing in the God full of grace enables such a look at and acceptance of human sin. Morality sees and accepts certain realities revealed in the Bible and experienced in life:

- doubts about God being full of grace, about Christ and his unconditional acceptance, about his constant presence and his faithfulness to his promises;
- a sense of omnipotence, the desire to want to be God and be in control of one's own life and the universe, the inability and refusal to completely let go and let God be God, the egocentricity, the wanting and expecting that life will spin around oneself with oneself in the center, the wanting of "my will be done" and "my kingdom come," the resistance to receiving that part of the life of Christ that turns life over to the care and will of the God full of grace;
- moralizing with God, self and others;
- denial and self-deception regarding the truth about oneself;
- rationalizing personal attitudes, feelings, and behaviors that are un-Christlike;
- caring deeds left undone,

- finding scapegoats and blaming others;
- hurts left unforgiven and unhealed;
- holding onto regrets;
- lack of empathetic understanding of others;
- impatience;
- perfectionism, which blocks emotional and spiritual growth;
- prejudice, intolerance, and injustice towards others;
- impulsiveness;
- using others;
- abusing others;
- hanging onto low self-esteem.
- being too dependent on the approval and acceptance signals from others, which prevents independent/dependent relationship life and prevents being ultimately dependent on God;
- overindependency, which blocks being able to be a receiving and giving person in relationships with others;
- failure to worship God in spirit and truth;
- materialism that makes money, material things, and pleasure the primary goals of life;
- lack of generosity toward the needs of others;
- putting success needs before faithfulness and service;
- not affirming and accepting responsibility to be stewards and enjoyers of God's creation;
- insensitivity and lack of concern for social justice;
- being unwilling to let go of one's egocentric self in order to find life.

There is much more, but that is a large part of the sin in our being. Most of that might be called immaturity by some, but it is more than that. It is our spiritual condition.

Morality doesn't moralize about it. Believing in the God full of grace, morality is the behavior that admits all sin, claims it as one's own, claims it individually and together. Morality steps into the presence of the God full of grace with all that sin and in boldness and confidence says, "This is me, and this is mine!" Morality confesses such sin in the behavior of faith in a God full of grace.

The morality of faith also affirms that sin isn't the whole story. Morality affirms and accepts the personhood, the dignity, the great value of oneself and others, who have been created in the image of God. Morality is a behavior that accepts the gospel's proclamation that in and by God's grace you are indeed a child of God—the crown of creation.

Morality is also the behavior of self-acceptance, self-affirmation, and self-esteem. Morality is the behavior of God's law of love towards oneself as well as others. If we don't have that love within and toward ourself, our relationships with others are impaired. Morality does not diminish oneself or another because of our common human sinfulness, our common brokenness and limitation. So it is that in relationship to self and others, morality is the behavior that affirms self and others as Christ affirms us.

In the Christian gospel morality is confession—accepting, acknowledging, being sorrowful for, wanting forgiveness for your sin and desiring to become more Christlike in relationship to God, self, and others. Confession is unfulfilled unless there is the desire and willingness to change. Changes in attitudes, feelings, and behavior will come only when there is acceptance of what needs to be changed. Acceptance deep within oneself is essential for change, and that acceptance is part of true confession. Change requires experiencing the pain and sorrow that comes from both the self-realization and the self-acceptance of one's personal violation of God's moral law of love in relationship to God, self, and others. Sin will never be removed in anyone's life or in this world. In this life there will never be perfection for anyone. None of us will attain the full maturity of the man Jesus in this life, but morality wants and seeks growth in that direction. The God full of grace never leads us around, but always leads us through what is and what needs to be changed, and that is often a painful path.

Morality accepts that "my will be done" will always be there. But morality is also the behavior of accepting and wanting, "Your will be done." Morality prays that prayer, not assuming it always knows the answer. Morality is the behavior of wanting to grow in the fruits of the spirit: love, joy, peace, patience, kindness, goodness, faithfulness, humility, and self-control.

Morality, Freedom, and Responsibility

Morality is the behavior of accepting the freedom for which Christ set us free. Morality is the behavior of assuming that freedom and being free of the burden of a moralistic, conditional, judgmental, and false god with all the moralistic rules.

In a day when there is a breaking down and tearing apart of what was perceived to be morality, many are left bewildered and frightened. Moral freedom seems to mean license. Apparently we thought we had morality put together and that it would stay the way we had it forever. But much of society has busted loose from that, and it appears to some that the moral structures are crumbling. Much of this seemingly radical change came as an inevitable reaction to moralism, because moralism is a misperception and violation of morality, of God's moral law of love. In that sense there can be something healthy going on.

But given this change, moralism is still active and vociferous in the church. The moralistic box in which moralism believes and lives is being held together and strengthened. And it is being done not only in the name of God but in the name of patriotism. Many are fleeing to the box to feel secure and shielded from the freedom and risks that come with the morality for which Christ frees us.

Morality is not the same as the moralistic box with its list of do's and don't's. Morality lives outside of that box in the world with its wonder and beauty, its pleasures and satisfactions, its sin and dirt, its joy and pain, its health and suffering, its hopes and disillusionments, its risks and failures, its living and dying. Morality moves out into the world freed up to assume responsibility for one's own attitudes, feelings, and behavior. No one else can be responsible for that. In order for there to be sanctification (change and growth) there has to be acceptance of that kind of life and personal responsibility.

Morality is being willing to live with the consequences of one's own attitudes, feelings, and behavior. In the living of life with such freedom there will always be both violations and fulfillments—and with them, growth. Now there is present not just "the flesh," but something new, which is the "spirit," the Spirit of our Lord, together with the promise and experience of his gracious presence and transforming power.

Morality is never totally individualistic, separate from others or God's creation. Morality is the behavior that seeks justice for the poor, for those who have committed crimes, for those who are discriminated against, for those who are the victims of racism. Morality bears one another's burdens, feeds the poor, comforts the lonely, and remembers the forgotten. Morality assumes responsibility for being stewards of the earth and the universe because it is God's and God's gift to his people. Morality seeks ways for peace and avoidance of violence and war.

Morality is the behavior of living free, not from the presence of guilt, but from the burden of guilt through faith in Christ.

Morality and Grace

The main thrust of morality is change and growth in Christlike faith, attitudes, and behaviors. Within that, morality accepts the condition of human limitation and the acceptance of that reality as essential to experience the sufficiency of God's grace. Only God can pronounce the final yes and no on your faith, attitudes, feelings, and behaviors, and God's yes and no are not always clear within the limitedness of our human condition. There are always ambiguities and inconsistencies. And knowing all this, morality lives the life of freedom and risk, assumes responsibility for violations of God's will, lives with the failures, and affirms the fulfillments, change, and growth, while trusting in the sufficiency of God's grace.

Morality accepts the fact that God will always *be* near but will not always *feel* near. Within the realities of aloneness and doubts is the abiding faith in God's grace and presence.

Morality seeks to accept others as they are and not with pretense based on what they might become. Morality is free to let others believe, think, and behave differently from oneself, while communicating by word and deed the God full of grace. Morality seeks to let others be responsible and live with the consequences of their behavior within the human environment of grace.

Morality seeks to communciate and share the good news of the gospel without manipulating or violating the personhood of others.

Morality is the father letting the son go, continuing to love him, waiting for his return, and welcoming him back with a big hug and a grand banquet.

Morality lovingly confronts and seeks to enable others to become aware of violations of love towards God, themselves, or others. Such confrontations may hurt, but emptied of moralism, they will not harm the persons involved. Morality is honest in relationships.

Morality is the behavior that is also open to such confrontation from others to learn to know oneself better and be open to the need for change in one's own attitudes, feelings, and behaviors.

Morality prays, "God grant me the serenity to accept the things I cannot change, courage to change the things I can, and wisdom to know the difference." Morality prays, "Not my will, but your will be done." There is no grace without morality, and no morality without grace.

CHAPTER NINE

Grace and Morality As Spirituality

The early members of A.A. had perceived God as being moralistic, judgmental, and condemning and therefore not a source of hope. They felt that if there was a God, that God had abandoned them. But in their recovery they came to realize that when they surrendered to their powerlessness over alcohol (their human limitation), God was there with them as a source of strength, hope, recovery, and a spiritual way of life with new meaning. God had not abandoned them; moralistic perception and reaction from church, society, and themselves had only made it feel that way. This experience of grace in their surrender took them out of the moralistic perception of God into a program of 12 moral steps that led them into a spiritual way of life. They had learned that spirituality had to do with experiencing surrender from omnipotence and egocentricity, coming to believe in a power greater than themselves, and turning their lives over to God's will and care as they understood him.

But they learned something else. They learned that spirituality is not and can never be just one-dimensional. They experienced that there is not only the divine involvement in spirituality but also the *human*. They experienced the *human environment of spirituality* in their nonmoralistic, understanding, accepting, and caring fellowship. There they could admit their pain, brokenness, and human limitation, and also experience human dignity and personal moral responsibility for attitudes, feelings, and be-haviors.

The word *morality* (emptied of moralism) and the word *spirituality* can be seen as interchangeable, but we choose the word *spirituality,* because it has more of the connotation of "a new way of life," of relation-ships and fellowship, of the person, message, and spirit of Christ, of the human environment together with the divine. It helps to make more clear that the ultimate reality in life with God, self, and others is the spiritual reality.

Four Dimensions of Spirituality

As I learned about spirituality in the nonreligious paradigm of A.A., I came to four conclusions.

1. *Spirituality and religion are not synonymous.*

A person can be very involved in religion or being religious and yet be lacking in spirituality. Many years ago a recovering Roman Catholic priest said, "Prior to my recovery in A.A. I was a very religious person and still am. But it was only through my recovery in A.A. that I found out what spirituality was all about."

In this priest's statement is a special message for clergy. Graduation from seminary and ordination into the ministry do not automatically carry with them the reality of spirituality. Evidence of that can be the continuing dominance of moralism or of the "omnipotent ego" and egocentricity in one's life-style, ministry, and relationships. Seminary graduation and ordination no more guarantee spirituality than graduation from medical school or a school of business administration.

A person not involved in religion can have considerable spirituality, as is true with some members of A.A. Of course, many religious people do have spirituality. Although spirituality is not uniquely Christian, there are in the spirituality of the gospel some unique realities.

Many recovering and nonrecovering alcoholics perceive religion, the church, and clergy as symbols of moralism. Therefore, we have to make it clear to alcoholics that when we are talking about spirituality, we are not necessarily talking about religion or being religious, because in their perception religion is synonymous with moralism, and moralism is always experienced as rejection. It offers them no hope for dealing with their pain, brokenness, and limitation.

2. *There is no moralism in spirituality.*

People in A.A. can be moralistic in various areas of their lives just like other people. In fact, as they talk about the spirituality in A.A., some of them can be very moralistic and nonspiritual in their remarks about the church. But *alcoholics as alcoholics* experience the spontaneous, warm, unconditional acceptance of spirituality within that fellowship.

They have painfully experienced their powerlessness over alcohol and a sense of hopelessness, individually and together. Within A.A. they have experienced a common source of help and hope in a higher power, and this has led them to find a new way of life together.

Often the church is not perceived or experienced as such an accepting human environment. When moralism dominates, there is no spirituality and no real Christian fellowship. When moralism dominates in the church, people do not feel they are understood or accepted as they are. In the Bible one essential mark of the church of Jesus Christ is a nonmoralistic, spontaneous, and warm human environment of spirituality—never perfect but truly present. Christ makes it clear that the fellowship of believers ought to know the difference between moralism and gracious acceptance, because they have seen, believed and are following him, the one who is full of grace in whom there is no moralism.

3. *There is no spirituality without morality.*

A.A. can help us understand how moralism interferes with spirituality. This fellowship maintains that the beginning of spirituality is letting go of the moralism about our condition and wholeheartedly accepting the reality of our human limitation and our responsibility in relationship to it. There is no starting point for spirituality other than nonmoralistic acceptance of human limitation.

Human limitation includes all our brokenness, alienation, and estrangement—the totality of what the Bible calls our sinful condition. Putting this biblical terminology into the context and terminology of the "powerlessness over alcohol" of A.A. and Kurtz's "essential human limitation" can help us in better understanding this aspect of our spiritual condition.

The *Chicago Tribune* carried an article on a prominent thoracic surgeon whose colleagues were appalled at his heavy smoking, and how he later totally denied his terminal lung cancer while continuing to smoke. He utterly denied his own human limitation and human vulnerability.

A pastor and spouse, a church council, and a bishop met to discuss the pastor's obvious alcoholism. The church council and bishop communicated no moralism, only understanding, acceptance, and the necessity for treatment. The firm denial of the pastor and the pastor's spouse revealed not only the denial of alcoholism but the denial of human limitation and vulnerability, even though the message of the gospel has at its core "essential human limitation."

While walking through a home for very sick elderly persons, I found myself saying to a friend, "Someday that could be us." Very quickly, however, that idea was placed in the denial file related to essential human limitation.

We respond to our powerlessness, our essential human limitation, by wanting to deny it while at the same time seeking to control it, fix it, eliminate it, and escape from it. But in A.A., people learned that facing their powerlessness, admitting it, accepting it, and assuming personal responsibility for responding to it in a nonmoralistic fellowship was the beginning of spirituality. And as people continue to come to the fellowship of A.A.—atheists, agnostics, Christians, and people of other faiths—they experience in this human environment that such surrender or acceptance is the beginning point for spirituality. And they know the difference between admitting human limitation and really accepting it or surrendering to it.

So we look again at the larger spiritual picture of life, which includes the totality of what the Bible calls our sinful condition. We look again at our not being God and wanting to be God, our inability to fully love our own selves and one another as Christ fully loves and accepts us, our need for redemption, our essential human limitation, our inability to control or change so many realities in life such as aging, dying, destruction by forces of nature, accidents, permanent disabling injury, terminal illness, disappointments, broken relationships, loss and grief. The gospel is the message that our God is with us, full of grace, for us and not against us. God calls us to surrender, to accept our human condition, alone and together, in this world as it is. That is essential in the spirituality of the Christian faith. The Bible makes it clear that there is no other beginning place. It is the moral imperative in spirituality.

As a nonreligious paradigm, A.A. members say that the next ingredient in spirituality, as they experienced it, was coming to believe that a power greater than themselves could restore them to sanity. They had experienced a sense of having been abandoned by a moralistic God, church, and society to live and die in their alcoholism. But as they surrendered to their human limitation, they came to believe in a power greater than themselves and discovered, to their surprise, that that power was present with them to support, strengthen, restore, and provide hope and a new life.

The message of the Christian religion to us in our human condition of sinfulness, of powerlessness and essential human limitation, is not only about a power greater than ourselves but about a God who has been revealed to us in person.

The Word became flesh and lived for a while among us. We have seen his glory, the glory of the one and only Son, who came from the Father, full of grace and truth (John 1:14).

"You are to give him the name Jesus, because he will save his people from their sins" (Matt. 1:21).

"Anyone who has seen me has seen the Father" (John 14:9).

"The work of God is this: to believe in the one he has sent" (John 6:29).

"I am the way and the truth and the life" (John 14:6).

Yet to all who received him, to those who believed in his name, he gave the right to become children of God (John 1:12).

"I am the resurrection and the life. He who believes in me will live, even though he dies; and whoever lives and believes in me will never die. Do you believe this?" (John 11:25-26).

The Christian gospel calls us to believe in Christ as our Lord, and in the sufficiency of his grace for all our needs, for all of life, for our death, and for our salvation. It calls us to put our ultimate trust in him for our salvation and change in our lives. This is the center of the spirituality of the gospel.

The founders of A.A. said that they had to decide to turn their lives over to the care of God as they understood him. This decision was essential to faith in God. They found this wasn't something that happened automatically. It was something they had to decide to do.

The Bible contains many statements regarding our need to let go of ourselves and commit our lives to Christ as the Lord of our lives. It calls us to stop seeking to do our own will and to commit our lives to the Lord to do his will. It speaks of the need to quit following other "gods" and to follow him. This is another essential reality in what our Lord describes as "being born anew" in relationship to our sinful condition, omnipotence, and egocentricity, our essential human limitation.

A.A. members also say that they needed to take a searching, fearless, moral inventory and admit to God, self, and another human being the exact nature of their wrongs. They found that was essential to their recovery. In fact, the early members of A.A. said that up until they did that, they had certain spiritual *beliefs,* but only afterwards did they begin to have a spiritual *experience.* That statement regarding this action of spirituality within our nonreligious paradigm is cause for us to reflect about confession in the Christian life.

Most Christians experience *general* confession in public worship—and this is good. But what about private confession, confessing to God, self, and *another human being*? In some churches people would announce privately to the pastor their intention of receiving Holy Communion. This private announcing to the pastor was recognition that "I have sinned" and, in some cases, included the confession of certain sins. The Roman Catholic church has had the sacrament of confession, and recently has reemphasized the need for private confession. Individual confession to another, in whatever shape or form, at times in life is indeed a valuable, if not essential, ingredient in spirituality. In his book *The Meaning of Persons,* Paul Tournier, a psychiatrist and a Christian, said that we become fully conscious only of what we are able to express to someone else.

Many people have confessed to God but then experienced no change or growth in that area of the Christian life. There can be many reasons for this. Sometimes the perceived sin and experienced guilt is distorted, neurotic, or obsessive. Sometimes people aren't ready to let go and change. But it can also be true that relief of guilt and change for some human realities won't occur as long as the confession is only to God. The person may not really be facing the sin; it remains "my secret" until it is confessed not only to God and self, but to another human being.

Having listened to many alcoholics individually admit to God, self, and another human being after taking a searching, fearless, moral inventory with the use of a moral inventory guide, I have become convinced that such "private confession" is indeed of real value, at certain times in life. There is value in it being done at least once in a thorough way. It is good to have someone who knows the truth about me as best I have come to know it through such an inventory. It may need to be repeated, if not for all areas of life, then maybe for certain ones. Once done formally, such private confession may then happen in an ongoing way within the warmth, intimacy, and trust of a marriage or family life or in a relationship with a pastor, counselor or friend. As with the other aspects of spirituality, a person may not understand the need and value of such private confession until the person does it. Private confession needs more attention in the Christian church.

After this step A.A. moves on to the moral behaviors of becoming willing to change, asking God's help to change, being forgiven by and forgiving others, forgiving self, seeking to remain honest with self, seeking greater knowledge of God's will and the power to do it, and sharing with others what has been received as a result of the spiritual awakening.

In their spiritual experience of recovery these A.A. pioneers learned basic moral principles and behaviors essential to the spiritual life. The spirituality of our Lord is built on the gracious law of love that is to be lived out in relationship to God, self, and others.

4. *Spirituality has to do with how we are met by God, how we meet our own selves, and how we meet each other.*

Although it is very personal, spirituality is not simply personal. It isn't something a person lacks and then suddenly receives from above. It isn't something involving only the person and a higher power, or God. Spirituality requires relationships—with God, with oneself, and with others. It is experienced and expressed in relationships. It has to do with how we are met by God and how we meet ourselves and each other in our essential human limitation (or in the language of the Bible, in our common sinful condition).

God's first meeting with us is usually in and through others. In A.A. spirituality is experienced within a fellowship of people who are emptied of moralism about alcoholism and have warm, genuine acceptance of the alcoholic. Such a human environment doesn't guarantee recovery, healing, and newness of life for every alcoholic who enters the door of an A.A. meeting, but it is essential if there is to be that experience of spirituality.

In that environment people hear, learn, and experience how God meets them in the reality of their human limitation. What they experience is not the conversion of the moralistic religionists, but the conversion to spirituality with new hope, new meaning, and new life. God meets them, is with them, accepts them in the midst of their powerlessness, and restores them with caring and strength within the fellowship of others, enabling them to grow spiritually,

The Christian church can learn a good deal in regard to the human environment of spirituality from the fellowship of A.A. Throughout history, the church has struggled with what it means to be the fellowship of believers in Christ. The Christian fellowship or community needs to express the nonmoralistic spirit of our Lord. Just as the Christian fellowship or community has the responsibility to preach and teach the gospel of our Lord, full of grace, so indeed it has the responsibility to incarnate the human environment of our Lord's spirituality. Within such an environment the Lord chooses to meet us through his Word and sacraments in our sinful human condition, our essential human limitation.

But A.A. also teaches us that spirituality involves meeting ourselves in our essential human limitation. If we don't meet ourselves there, we never meet ourselves, and we miss spirituality.

A.A. also makes clear that spirituality involves meeting each other in our essential human limitation with the awareness of our human dignity and value. If we don't meet each other in that way, we never really meet or experience a spiritual union. We can know each other for years as friends, colleagues, spouses, parents or children, but if we don't meet each other in our essential human limitation, we never meet. There is not only the divine-human vertical dimension to spirituality; there is this human to human-horizontal dimension. Within the Christian faith this is symbolized by the cross.

Let me use the International A.A. convention in Miami some years ago to clarify what is meant by meeting each other in our human limitation. As a nonalcoholic, I saw people from all over North America and from other parts of the world meeting for the first time—one individual with another—and as soon as they met they knew each other. They knew each other because within the fellowship they had mystically already met and now they were meeting personally in the common reality of their essential human limitation. Out of the common pain of their human limitation they had found a common hope and a new life. They didn't know everything about one another. But they mutually had experienced and accepted the powerlessness of the human condition. It happened in a human fellowship as they experienced together the human-to-human dimension of spirituality.

Spirituality in Christian Context

I want to add one nonalcoholic example that gives clear expression to the content and experience of these dimensions of spirituality.

I have come to have very high regard for Joseph Cardinal Bernardin, Archbishop of Chicago. He lives and communicates a deep sense of spirituality. The book *The Spirit of Cardinal Bernardin* by A. E. P. Wall (Chicago: Thomas More, 1983), quotes some statements the cardinal made to 150 Chicagoland priests involved in Hispanic ministry. Cardinal Bernardin spoke about a profound spiritual change that took place in his life. He told the priests that he had been ordained nearly 31 years, and,

It took me nearly twenty-five years to realize that my busyness wasn't really what the Lord and the people wanted (no matter how many demands the latter seemed to be making). It took me nearly twenty-five years to realize that, if I wanted to be a truly successful priest and bishop, I had to put Jesus first in my life—not merely in theory but in practice.

It was about six years ago—with the help of some priests—all younger and holier than I—that I learned how to pray. It was then that I let go of Joe Bernardin and grabbed on to the Lord. And since that time everything has changed.

And then he went on to say this, just like the woman patient who talked of her surrender to Dr. Tiebout,

Don't misunderstand: the human condition which I share with you and everyone else has not disappeared. Externally, my responsibilities—the pressures—have increased. Internally, I confront the same difficulties as before. I must come to grips with my sexuality and what it means for me as one who has committed himself to celibacy for the sake of the Kingdom. I experience loneliness at times, despite a life crowded with people and events.

I experience anxieties caused by a fear that I will not live up to others' expectations. My feelings are hurt when others misunderstand or criticize what I do. I am frustrated when my best efforts seem to accomplish little or nothing. I am plagued at times by a certain spirited dryness or aridity, a sense of abandonment—even when I am desperately searching for the Lord in prayer. I suffer a loss of morale when people seem to not notice what I am doing. When they take me for granted. So the human condition has not changed. I experience all the same difficulties as before.

He went on to talk about how he had learned to deal better with the difficulties.

Now it is no longer, I alone. It is the Lord and I, together. Indeed it is my weakness and vulnerability that become my strength because then I no longer pretend that I am in control, but the Lord Jesus.

In the final analysis, the Cardinal said,

. . .my best contribution or gift is to help you grow in the Lord who alone can bring your efforts to fruition. My best gift to you is myself. Beneath the titles of archbishop or cardinal is a man—Joseph Bernardin—who is weak and sinful like you, in need of affirmation and support, at times full of doubts and anxieties, very sensitive, easily hurt and frustrated.

But this Joseph Bernardin is also a man of great faith, one who is in love with the Lord, one who struggles each day—sometimes with little obvious success—to decrease so the Lord can increase in him, a man whose life is full of crooked lines but who is willing to let the Lord write straight with them. My brothers, know that this man, Joseph, has a great affection for you. Know that when you fail, he understands. Know that when you do crazy things that bring grief to others (as he himself does so frequently), he forgives you. Know that as you try to cope with the realities of life—both personally and ministerially—he is at your side, ready to help in every way he can.

Know that when you succeed, he smiles and shares your joy and satisfaction. Know that when you are sad, hurt, demoralized, he cries with you. Know that this man, Joseph, loves you; that he is proud of you; and that, for the sake of the Lord, he is ready and willing to give his life for you!

That is a clear and evangelical description of spirituality within as revealed in Christ—his life, his cross and resurrection. It describes how we are met by our Lord and how we meet ourselves, and each other within the kingdom of God.

Two Approaches to Growth

Emotional and spiritual growth need to be discussed in relationship to two approaches. One is prominent in the church and the other in the psychotherapy and counseling.

There is the approach in some churches that only prayer is necessary for emotional or spiritual problems. Everything is perceived and responded to as direct intervention by the Lord. If what is prayed for doesn't happen, the answer is weakness of faith or the need for "being converted" or "being saved." This approach ignores many aspects of spirituality.

Then there is the purely humanistic approach to change and growth. This has often aimed at helping people get in touch with their poor self-image and feelings of inferiority and moving them to greater self-affirmation. Those are basic human needs and values, but that isn't the way for people to get to self-esteem and self-affirmation. The best that I have seen from such an approach is that some people are able to make some adjustment or modification, but the basic problems linger on.

Dr. Tiebout was aware of the importance of addressing poor self-image and feelings of inferiority, but he said that lurking underneath is the problem of the "omnipotent ego." It is beyond conscious awareness, buried within and disguised. To get over the poor self-image and feelings of inferiority, the person would have to become perfect, with the sense of complete control and "having it my way" demanded by the omnipotent ego and the egocentric self. And when you turn over the low self-image and feelings of inferiority and look at the other extreme expression of it, that is exactly what you see. You see the "omnipotent ego," the sense of being the great exceptional achiever, and the need to be in control. You see the big exaggerated "I" and the bondage to its domination.

In spirituality it is essential that the helper has high esteem for the person who comes with low self-esteem. The helper must see the person who has a low self-image as a person created in the image of God and having great value. The helper must be sensitive to and accepting of the way the person so negatively perceives himself or herself. The helper must be able to begin where the person is, to be genuine, empathic, warm, honest, and open, and in this way to provide the human environment of spirituality.

Over time and in appropriate ways people need to get in touch with their essential human limitation, vulnerability, alienation, and the dominant "omnipotent ego" and egocentricity. It is important that there be movement towards that which the Bible and our Lord nonmoralistically call our imperfection, our rebellion against God, our wanting to be God, and our perfectionism and self-deception.

Such movement usually requires time and comes in bits and pieces, as does most movement toward self-awareness and emotional and spiritual growth. Some persons are so badly damaged that they aren't able to move in this direction at all. They may have primary, permanent impairment in their thinking processes. They may have severe chronic psychiatric disorder. They may have severe damage to self-worth and self-esteem, as seen in some depression. However, in regard to the latter, within the human environment of spirituality in a long-term treatment process, more of these people could come to the awareness of the need for a surrender than some professionals think.

Over time in treatment some can become keenly aware of the real nature of their pain. They can come to understand and accept that there are reasons why they are depressed. They can come to understand and accept that some of the pain will resurface at certain vulnerable times, triggering off the old reactions. But they can also come to understand and accept that such pain and reactions need no longer dominate their lives.

They can become aware of the sense of omnipotence and egocentricity common to us all, which had been out of conscious awareness because of the pain of their depression. They can then come to the awareness of the need to accept who and what can't be changed, and get involved in changing what can be changed. While experiencing healing within the human environment of spirituality in treatment, they can begin to experience meaning, change, growth, and hope that brings with it a growing sense of self-worth and self-esteem.

When they are able to surrender to the pain, brokenness, and human limitation, they too can discover that this is the beginning of spiritual awakening, newness of faith, new behaviors, new commitments, new values, new life.

Psychiatry, psychology, and social work can help us understand human nature and how individuals and families can be helped. However, they can provide little more than modifications and adjustments unless they integrate the spiritual dimension, like A.A.

The spiritual dimension of life needs to be included in nonreligious counseling and treatment services. Only it can deal with the inner sense of omnipotence that is by nature dominant within us. It has to do with our essential human limitation and our being non-God. It has to do with our egocentric center. Something needs to be changed and made new in that inner core. It needs more than modification or adjustment. It has to do with needed change that humans can't make happen and requires coming to believe in a power greater than oneself. And for this, humans need the human environment of spirituality, whether offered within or outside the church, within or outside a religious context. Augustine summed up this reality of the human condition by saying, "Our souls are restless until they rest in thee, O God."

Growth and Pain

On this journey I also learned that perfectionism is an unhealthy spiritual reality. It blocks growth. By contrast, the spirituality of the gospel focuses on change and growth in faith and life. If, because of perfectionism, we are always dissatisfied, wanting to be beyond where we are, we will never get there. A basic ingredient in spirituality is gratitude, for what has been received, for the growth that has taken place. This gratitude opens the way for new growth. There can be no real gratitude within perfectionism.

Emotional and spiritual growth always involves pain. It involves the willingness to experience the pain of certain insights about oneself, the pain of risking oneself with others, the pain of disillusion-ment with self and others, the pain of doing the thing never done before that is necessary to experience growth, the pain of taking that first step with others. It involves the pain of becoming aware of our own omnipotence, egocentricity, and estrangement from God. It involves seeing our self-deception. It involves the fear of letting go and entrusting life to God. Through all kinds of ways, including religion, people seek to avoid or diminish the pain essential for emo-tional and spiritual growth. It is because growth in-volves pain that Dr. M. Scott Peck entitled his book, *The Road Less Traveled*. And it is also because of this pain that the human environment of spirituality is essential for self with others.

The Bible often refers to the pain in life as an inescapable reality. In spirituality one abandons the search for an answer to the *why* of pain. The gospel's response to the problem of suffering can be summarized in three commands: (1) trust in God's grace, abiding presence, and his promise that all pain can work for good in our life; (2) deny yourself, take up your cross, and follow Christ, (3) bear one another's burdens. The Bible and our own Christian experience teach us there is no other way to find healing, meaning, growth, and hope in the midst of pain, brokenness, and human limitation.

Much of the pain and suffering in life is evil, and not of God's creation or design. But as Douglas John Hall has noted, some struggle and pain may be built into creation and therefore is of God. In Christian spirituality we are called to accept all pain and suffering as part of the realities of life, but not as the final word. Because God bears our pain with us and as we bear one another's pain, we are assured of meaning and hope, spiritual growth, and, strangely enough, even gratitude. Pain, suffering, and death are not the final word. The final word is our Lord. He will see us through in his abiding and eternal love.

As Christ took on our pain, so we are to do that with and for others. This is not to be done in such a way that the pain of others overwhelms us, making us captive to their pain and unable to live freely our own lives. But we are to identify with, feel, and carry one another's pain. There is no way to bear another's burden objectively and analytically. Such thinking in the professional helping field is both distortion and myth. Also, in order for us to be involved in sharing and bearing the pain of others, we need to share our pain with others so they can bear our pain with us.

The way of love, of obedience, of growth, the way of following him who is the Way, the Truth, and the Life is a way of pain. But with the pain of life there can also be joy, satisfaction, celebration, gratitude, and strengthening of faith through learning the sufficiency of God's grace, learning that surely God's goodness and mercy go with us all the days of our lives.

The Problem of Fixation

In learning about spirituality from A.A., I also observed that a person can have a profound spiritual experience related to surrender to the powerlessness over alcohol and a life that had become unmanageable, but end up having the experience get fixated around alcoholism. What was received in the spiritual experience is not extended into the other areas of the person's life. It gets encapsulated into the singular phenomenon of "I am an alcoholic and by the grace of God I am sober," and the person's relationships are totally alcoholism oriented.

A corollary might be the individual or church body that ends up with a rigid, highly dogmatic belief system that dominates all life and is perceived as being the ultimate reality. Another could be focusing on only one aspect of the Bible or Christian faith, or on one religious experience, in such a way that all Christianity gets encapsulated into that. A person can have an initial meaningful experience in spirituality and have it become fixated. In some cases this can be related to serious psychological or psychiatric problems.

The Language and the World of People

I also came to see that the language of spirituality is important. It is not only spiritual language; it is the language of the people. Christian spirituality, too, does not have to be expressed only in the language of the Bible or Christian theology. Martin Luther understood this so well. A deeply spiritual person who regularly used the spiritual language of the Bible and Christian theology, Luther also was of the people and frequently expressed his spirituality in very earthy language, the language of the people. Just as there is spiritual language in spirituality, so there is the language of the people. Such language is part of the human environment of spirituality.

Spirituality is lived and expressed in the world with all the various human situations and conditions. The life of Jesus makes that so clear. Spirituality is being with people where they are and as they are, not only in those places and situations that someone within the church has dogmatically defined as "being Christian." Nor is it entering those places and situations identified as "non-Christian" to communicate in a moralistic way a message of "Jesus saves." Spirituality is being with people in the midst of the distortion of life and meaning

Spirituality is also enjoying the goodness of God's created world and creative people. Spirituality is being fully in the world, enjoying and participating in a variety of situations and experiences.

Sharing with Others

A.A. emphasizes the need to share with others what has been received through a spiritual awakening. A.A. members know that to keep it only for oneself is to lose it. But they do not go out to share it with others unless they are asked to do so through a phone call or personal contact. From their spiritual experiences outside formal religion they have learned that spirituality involves both the need and desire to share with others the newness, strength, and hope they have received.

And so it is with all spirituality. However, within the context of the Christian message there is our Lord's command to go into all the world and share the good news. In seeking to fulfill that command, we need to create the human environment of spirituality. Moralism not only distorts the reality of spirituality within the Christian church; it just plain "messes up" the mission.

Our Lord identified so closely with those in pain, loneliness, and poverty that he said, "Whatever you do for them, you do for me." The gospel joins us to people in need—whether they are or are not of the faith and with no strings attached. Spirituality in the gospel context necessitates concern and involvement in issues of social justice, not always knowing for certain what is right, but seeking to communicate what we believe to be the mind and spirit of our Lord.

Giving of self and one's resources for others is another basic ingredient of spirituality in the gospel. Without such giving there is no spirituality. The identification of the Lord as our servant and our call to be servants are inescapable, and servanthood includes our money. Generosity with one's resources is one of the hallmarks of spirituality in the Bible.

Personal Involvement

Spirituality requires personal involvement evidenced in personal decision making and behavior. It requires decision translated into behavior. One cannot just think or feel one's way into spirituality. In the Twelve Steps A.A. members talk about what they *need to do*. To not do is to never know and never experience and never live the life of spirituality. The Bible also emphasizes that only in doing can we know, and only in doing can there be change and growth.

Prayer in Spirituality

As part of their spirituality A.A. members pray two prayers—the Lord's Prayer and the Serenity Prayer:

God grant me the serenity to accept the things I cannot change, courage to change the things I can, and wisdom to know the difference.

Such prayers are also essential in Christian spirituality.

Confrontation with Death

As we journey through life in the Christian faith, our Lord keeps confronting us with the reality of our sinful condition—our pain, brokenness, and human limitation. He keeps calling us to accept it as reality with the assurance that his abiding gracious presence and strength are sufficient for all our need. And as he does this, he keeps confronting us with the last great human limitation, which is death. To become reconciled with our own death, as well as the death of family members and friends, is essential in spirituality. Christian spirituality calls us to live with, affirm, and express the pain, the doubts, the hurt, the anger, the fear, the grief, and whatever else we feel when we face our own death or the death of a loved one. That is strength, not weakness, and life teaches us that working through all that takes time.

But within that there is faith in the great good news of Easter. Jesus says, "Fear not. I live, and because I live you will live also." He calls us to become reconciled with death, to believe that he has conquered death, and to trust that he will go with us in it and through it. Spirituality within the gospel includes believing that then "we shall be like him, for we shall see him as he is" (1 John 3:2). Paul says, "Now we see but a poor reflection; then we shall see face to face. Now I know in part; then I shall know fully, even as I am fully known (1 Cor. 13:12). We will experience that fulfillment with God, self, and others in a new heaven and a new earth. In the spirituality of the gospel the ultimate is trust in our Lord, committing not only our living but also our dying to

him—the resurrected one, full of grace and always
with us.

On the cross Jesus exclaimed, "Father, into your
hands I commit my spirit" (Luke 23:46). In life and
in death our Lord is the ultimate expression of true
spirituality. And to those who confess his name he
says, "Follow me."

On my journey I have been strengthened in the
faith that in our pain, brokenness and human limitation, in the reality of our sinful condition, Jesus,
the one full of grace, indeed is the Way, the Truth,
and the Life.

CHAPTER TEN

Reflections on Christian Themes

The Word "Sin"

The word *sin* is an important word in the Bible, the only word that describes the basic spiritual nature of persons outside the reality and presence of God's grace. The church has never abandoned this word, even though at times it has felt uncomfortable, even apologetic, about it. Critics outside the church have called it a terrible word, and even within the church, people have said that there has been too much focus on sin.

Within the context of God's love and grace, sin has never been a bad word. It has always been a good word—good in the sense that it alone describes the inability of humans to let God be God, the inability of humans to fulfill God's moral law of love by perfectly loving God, oneself, and others, the inability to heal our own brokenness or remove our human limitation. Sin is not a terrible mark to put on people; it is an honest mark identifying a human spiritual reality.

The problem has never really been with the word *sin,* but with the moralistic content associated with it. Just as moralism distorts and diminishes the word *grace,* so moralism also distorts the word *sin.* Sin is a gracious word from our God that honestly communicates the nature of our spiritual condition and the necessity of God's gracious activity in the incarnation and in sending of the Holy Spirit.

The word *sin* in no way diminishes the dignity or worth of our personhood. The hymn with the moralistic phrase, "for such a worm as I," needs to be revised or else removed from all hymnals. In our moralistic response we may sometimes feel as if we are of no worth and dignity, but that is never true. Sin never removes the reality of being persons created in the image of God. The church has a responsibility to empty this good word *sin* of moralism in order to communicate it as a gracious word about a serious and painful reality of our lives, for which, thank God, he has revealed his grace as redemptive and sufficient.

The Name of Jesus

Jesus is the name above every name, a name full of grace. However, both in the parish ministry and in specialized ministry in alcoholism, I have observed problems in effectively communicating that name. Many within the church do not perceive Jesus as an unqualifiedly good name in their faith and experience. Both in the proclamation of his name and in the reception of that proclamation, moralism has been the source of problems. Many in pulpit and pew see in this unconditional name of grace a conditional God. Many perceive Jesus not as full of grace, but as conditional, judgmental, and condemning.

Many have left the church because such an understanding of Jesus has alienated them. Others have remained but have detached themselves from regularly hearing the proclamation of his name in worship. Both groups think that if the love of Jesus is conditional, they can live a good life apart from worship. When God's grace in Jesus is perceived as conditional on our behavior, people may remove or distance themselves from the institutionalized church. Moralism can cause people to leave the church, or to flee to even more moralistic churches.

Within our churches and families we need to do a better job of communicating the proclamation of the name of Jesus so that for more people it can indeed be the gracious name which is above every name. Human pain that is unheard or is responded to moralistically can sustain and feed the moralistic belief and perception of God. "Why me?" frequently has within it the cry of our moralistic belief and perception and needs to be heard as such. Surely in that moment and experience the name of Jesus is not the good name above every name. It is then a name associated with a moralistic, conditional, judgmental, and punishing God.

When I entered ministry in alcoholism, I soon learned that the name of Jesus was not a good, hope-filled name for most alcoholics. Most of them were raised within the church, but for them the name was filled with moralism, judgment, and condemnation. Many of those raised in the church even had trouble with the term "power greater than ourselves" in the Twelve Steps of A.A. Moralism empties the name of Jesus of its great beauty, goodness, and grace.

As we better proclaim his good name in word, sacrament, and deed, we should not assume that people will flock to the Christian church. The Bible declares that the crucified and risen Jesus will always be a stumbling block. Within our being is that which does not want to believe in such a one or any need for such a one. We want to believe that if there is any need for redemption, we can accomplish it for ourselves by our own goodness. We want to believe we can make our own truth, our own way, our own life.

But to have the name and person of Jesus emptied of moralism simply means that Jesus himself will be the stumbling block rather than the moralism attached to his name. The moralistic proclamation of Jesus prevents people from having to come face to face with Jesus as he has revealed himself.

The church needs to graciously proclaim with courage that moralism is not the good news in any way, shape, or form. The good news is, "For God so loved the world that he gave his one and only Son, that whoever believes in him shall not perish but have eternal life" (John 3:16). The next verse is also essential: "For God did not send his Son into the world to condemn the world, but to save the world through him" (v.17). Saving is the personal activity of a God full of grace, a God of unconditional love. And his name is Jesus, the name above every name. Jesus is the Lord, full of grace.

What a difficult command and task to effectively communicate the nature of sin and the nature of grace as revealed in Jesus—the nonmoralistic one! But the command has been given, and the task is ours. We, the moralistic ones, are to proclaim the glory of his name and the wonder of his grace in faith, word, and deed in our churches, in our families, and in our relationships with others. For that task he assures us that his grace will be sufficient.

The Lord's Prayer

The Lord's Prayer is a gift of grace. "Our Father" is Jesus' declaration, his communication, his assurance to us and for us that his grace is unconditional. There are no strings attached, no qualifications. This we believe and proclaim through faith in the Word who became flesh and dwelt among us. "Our Father"—he says it for us and gives it to us.

"Hallowed be your name, your kingdom come, your will be done on earth as it is in heaven" (Matt. 6:9-10). The omnipotence and egocentricity are still within us but no longer dominate and control our life. Jesus' spirit now also dwells within us and enables us to want God to be the God of life, to want God at the center, to want God's name hallowed, God's kingdom to come, and God's will to be done in our own lives, in the lives of others, and in our life together.

That is the fulfilling of the moral law of love. That is having life and having it abundantly.

"Give us today our daily bread." We recognize that God is the source and provider, that all material goodness comes from him. It is not just for me but for us. We don't pray egocentrically and selfishly for *my* material needs," but for *ours*; there is to be sharing. And we pray not for what we want in the future, but for what we need today.

"Forgive us our debts, as we also have forgiven our debtors" (Matt. 6:12). Forgiveness of self and others is unconditional love like his love for us. There is no forgiveness without that kind of love. Forgiveness of others is evidence both of love for another and oneself. It is obedience to God's moral law of love, loving one another as God loves us.

"And lead us not into temptation, and deliver us from the evil one" (Matt. 6:13). Graciously he affirms to us and allows for us the same prayer he prayed in the garden, "My Father, if it be possible, may this cup be taken from me" (Matt. 26:39). How totally he incorporates our basic human condition! How utterly human he allows and asks us to be! As our example he demonstrated that there is no evil for which God's grace is insufficient. He asks us to pray as those who believe that whatever trials and evil we experience, our God is present with us. He will sustain us in our faith and assure us that he has indeed conquered all evil. Nothing is capable of separating us from his love we have in Christ Jesus. Truly, "The kingdom, the power and the glory are yours, now and forever. Amen."

The Lord's Supper

The Lord's Supper is for us the purest expression of his grace, his unconditional love. The fact that the Lord's Supper is wrapped in mystery can be a problem, but at the same time it makes crystal clear that believing in his grace as revealed in the Incarnation is indeed always a matter of faith and mystery.

How thoughtful of our Lord. How filled with grace is his instituting and leaving for us the Lord's Supper. What more can he say and do?

As we share in the Lord's Supper, we hear his gracious words, "This is my body, given for you. This is the new covenant in my blood shed for you and for all people for the forgiveness of sins." There are no strings attached, no conditions, no qualifications, no "shouldisms." He institutes this grace-filled mystery. He uses bread and wine, symbols of food and drink, of fellowship, of being together. And he says, "Do this to remember me in faith—full of grace—my body and blood shed for you."

And when we do this and remember him, we are mystically but truly in communion with the whole body of his people. As he meets us in our brokenness with his own brokenness for us, we meet each other in our mutual brokenness. We are the ever-forgiven who are to be ever-forgiving. We are to feel the pain of one another and the need for one another. We are to respond in love like his toward one another. We are to be grace-full with and for one another. We are to share the wonder and glory of being called the children of God by faith.

Postscript

Some years ago I was sitting in the living room with my Grandma Sackman—my mother's mother. She was in her 70s. We were talking about God's grace revealed in Christ, the trustworthiness of the message and the promises. At that point this was solidly embedded in her faith. And while not simplistic, her faith was genuinely and magnificently simple.

On her journey in life there had been severe physical hardships on the prairies of South and North Dakota. There had been significant emotional and spiritual pain, including the death of their oldest daughter in the flu epidemic in 1917 and my grandfather's alcoholism. But in and through it all her faith was strengthened and life now was entrusted to the Lord as she continued to work in a home for the elderly. From this uneducated, theologically unsophisticated person I heard one of the most meaningful and profound expressions of the Christian

faith. When asked how she came to such an awareness and belief in the grace of God in Christ she
simply said, "It is so clear and simply stated in the
Bible." She knew through faith that Christ was her
Lord and that the purpose of life was to seek to do
his will. Human omnipotency and egocentricity
would be words too big for her to understand. But
clearly they were not dominating her life. At the center was Christ and service to others. That is what
gave meaning and hope to her living and dying.

I mention Grandma Sackman to bring into focus
the fact that the gospel of God's grace revealed in
Christ is indeed a simple message. Christ himself
said, ". . . anyone who will not receive the kingdom
of God like a little child will never enter it" (Mark
10:15). Not childishness, but childlikeness is essential in believing and living the gospel of our Lord. In
the history of the church there has been a host of
people who have lived and died in simple, childlike,
and yet profound faith. A person such as Christina
Sackman reminds us that faith is not so much a matter of *knowing* as it is believing, trusting, risking,
and following. She knew that the secret to life in the
midst of pain, brokenness, and human limitation is
really no secret at all.